HIDDEN GOLD
The Seventh Question

Uncle Al & Lynda,

May you always

find gold !

Tyssa Newton-Tessa

December 2006

HIDDEN GOLD
The Seventh Question

Written and Illustrated By
Teresa Newton-Terres

TNT Press
A Division of Project-TNT, LLC

HIDDEN GOLD
The Seventh Question

www.TNTPress.com

www.Project-TNT.com

Cover and Content Illustrations Copyright © 2006 by Teresa Newton-Terres

ISBN-13: 978-0-9791447-0-7
ISBN-10: 0-9791447-0-1

Christmas Edition Printing, December 2006

Summary:
Sixth grader Kenny Newton must interview Old Man Eagle to discover the secrets
of the mysterious garage and the source of the words that have echoed in his
thoughts ever since the car crash that killed his mother and baby sister. Kenny
learns some of life's lessons as he discovers the liquid gold of kings.

For Harold J. Newton,

Who inspired me with Proverbs 24:13-14.

CONTENTS

⊚ Acknowledgments ⊚

For a lifetime of inspiration, I thank my daughter Dete…as well as her brother and sister, Jon and Jessica and my dear grandchildren: Alexandrea, Andrew, Sarah, and Haven. And I appreciate the many who contributed to this projects effort: Bubba Sims, Diego Terres III, Diego Terres IV, Eva Hedricks, Lauren Reams, Shawn Hepler, and Derek Fleming. Most of all, I thank Ken for filling my life with faith, family, friends and living wild at heart.

◎ Forward ◎

HIDDEN GOLD is not a true story yet, there are many truths within its pages: there is a mysterious garage built of Cypres planks; there was an Old Man Eagle that pursued a family avocation inside that garage; there is an old man, Harold J., who was a Railway "Super" Postman and treasured liquid gold; and there is a young man Kenny who learned many lessons hidden inside that weather-beaten garage.

The author is a spouse to an Active Duty Army Officer for the National Guard Bureau. This story was inspired during one of the families moves when challenged by change and living in temporary housing between Washington DC, California, Pennsylvania, Kansas, Hawaii and Arkansas.

This is a special Christmas Edition of HIDDEN GOLD. This work is much like the three and four year old children who sang Christmas Songs today at a ladies Bible study luncheon... they were so young that their performance was unique and divinely entertaining! Parents lined the back of the room with their cameras to record the cherished memory. Likewise, this publication is a milestone to celebrate...Enjoy.

•1•
THE STAKE-OUT

"I'm not hungry!" Kenny yelled from his upstairs room as he got ready for school. It took him longer to get ready for school than most kids his age. He liked a buttoned shirt, and buttoned each button. He made his bed and smoothed out all the wrinkles. Before leaving his room, Kenny ran down a mental checklist: floor cleared, drawers pushed in, TV and computer turned off, homework in backpack. Kenny tried to do things right. His mother hadn't.

Each year Kenny seemed to take longer and longer getting ready for school, and now that he was in the sixth grade he took so long he had no time for breakfast.

"You come down and eat this breakfast I cooked for you! Think of the starving children around the world!" Kenny's grandmother said.

"Send it to them!" Kenny answered as he turned off his bedroom light.

"I see those friends of yours," said Grandmother,

looking out at Pedro and ET strolling from their house toward hers.

Kenny sprang down the stairs and grabbed his lunch out of his grandmother's hand. Grandmother stood at the front door holding out a warm, honey-drizzled biscuit and Kenny's designer lunch bag. "Thanks Grandmother!" said Kenny. Beside her stood Blondie, Kenny's golden retriever, a medium size dog with floppy ears and a long furry tail.

"Bye Blondie, bye girl!" He crouched, swung an arm around her thick collared neck, and squeezed her tightly. Blondie's tongue landed a slobbery kiss on his cheek. "Stop that! Kenny cried, wiping slime clear with his hand. "You know I don't like messy dog kisses."

"I'll be back from school before you know it, girl!" Kenny announced. Blondie lunged, but grandmother had taken a firm hold of her collar. "No escaping me, Blondie," said Grandmother. Blondie's tail beat repeatedly against Grandmother's leg.

"That top shirt button will stop the blood flowing to your brain," Grandmother said.

"You're supposed to use them!" said Kenny. Grandmother looks like a pink powder puff, he thought. "Nice robe!" said Kenny as he slipped past her and out the door. Grandmother loves anything that comes through mail delivery, thought Kenny.

"It is the latest thing!" Grandmother smiled as she swayed back and forth. "You be careful about picking up bad habits from them immigrants," grandmother called to Kenny.

Kenny cringed, rolled his eyes, and hoped Pedro and his little sister didn't hear her. Grandma's old fashioned, Kenny thought. Elizabeth Trinidad or ET as the kids all called her was just a kid in kindergarten. And Pedro was different, but not because his mother came from Mexico, had skin that looked tanned, or wore the same ball hat day after day. Pedro was Pedro, always trying to be somebody. Who? Pedro hadn't figured that out yet. Once he was going to be a baseball pro, until he broke Grandmother's front window with his fastball. Then he was going to be a doctor, until he sat in Piney Principal's office because he used a doctor's stethoscope to hear girls' heart beat. Last week he was going to be a preacher, until he was beat up for quoting the Bible and condemning the school bullies to a life in hell. Pedro's okay, he just acts before he thinks, and gets into trouble. Sometime he gets me into trouble too, thought Kenny.

"What's that hanging on your neck?" Kenny called, as he ran up to Pedro and ET.

"Dad's binoculars," Pedro replied, lifting them to

his eyes and getting close to Kenny's face. "Something's up at Old Man Eagle's. I was checking out the old man's garage last evening. Weird boxes! Dark jugs! A strange golden glow! Spooky mist! And there was a huge monster in the mist! "

"Why didn't you call me?" Kenny asked.

"I tried!" Pedro exclaimed. "Your grandmother answered your cell and said it was too late for good boys to talk." He scrunched his nose to mimic grandmother's words.

That's grandmother, thought Kenny. "Your dad let you take his binoculars?"

"Yeah, I'm going to be an Explorer! And with these we can really check out what the old man is up to!" Pedro peered through the binoculars. "Wow! Check out that booger in your nose, Kenny!"

Kenny pushed the binoculars out of his face, "You know, it gives me the heeby geebys to cross Old Man Eagle's property." A chill rippled through him as he thought of his grandmother's familiar words, "Your mother and sister would still be alive if Mr. Eagle had let the city build a straight road through Eagle property."

"Get over it! You don't want the old man to cause more trouble do you?" Pedro taunted, as he set out.

"What's on your lunch sack today?" ET asked,

tugging at Kenny's elbow.

Kenny held out his lunch sack. "Pink polka-dots!" ET said. "Your Grandma gets the best bags."

Another mail delivery, thought Kenny.

"Johnny, the kid in the chair behind me in class, is going to give me trouble for this one," he winked at ET as he hid the sack.

"Come on," Pedro said as he took off. His long legs carried him easily over the rail and wire fence of Old Man Eagle's property. Kenny boosted ET over and then crossed the barrier himself. Tall grass rustled with each of their steps. It was a short cut, but Kenny didn't like to take it very often. Kenny's back shivered with each step across Eagle's property. Dark clouds began gathering in the sky and floated in front of the sun, a darkness spread around them.

"Kenny, why are you scared of the Eagle property?" ET asked, she huffed and puffed, out of breath from keeping up with the boys.

"Shut up ET! I said you can come with us, if you don't talk," Pedro answered. At times, Pedro is too bossy, thought Kenny. I don't mind ET tagging along. She's the same age as Sissy.

Even after three years Kenny was still piecing together that evening. If his mother had only called

before leaving and found out that the school's open house was postponed because of bad weather, they could have stayed home that night. Instead, they started out in a hurry because mother thought they were going to be late. It was raining hard, trees were swaying in the wind, the sky had an eerie dark green glow -- the old car's brakes went out, right at the curve and their car flew off the road. Kenny remembered Grandmother's words, you were found outside the car, but your Mom and Sissy died when the car crashed into the big tree at the edge of Old Man Eagle's property.

"Mom and Sissy died near here," Kenny frankly said. "I don't remember much. Except -- it was dark and then there was a bright flash of light.   What he didn't say was, a voice continues to haunt him, "The Lord will keep you from harm... ,The Lord   will keep you from harm..., The Lord will keep you from harm." His mother's last breaths? An angel's voice? God's? The words echoed in his thoughts on dark nights, when he is scared, and on touching Eagle's property. Kenny saw a tear trickled down ET's cheek. He said no more about it.

"You got to see the old man's garage," Pedro said. "Things are hanging on it, leaning against it, laying around it, and has whirling noises bellowed out of it."

"Things are always around it."

"This is different!" Pedro argued.

They darted behind bushes and trunks as they went up the ridge overlooking Old Man Eagle's house and garage. "See those dark jugs and the tall coffin-boxes," Pedro said, as he pointed his finger toward the garage, and handed the binoculars to Kenny.

"Hum" Kenny peered through the binoculars.

"It's a coffin, right!" Pedro whispered.

"Coffins aren't put on their end. They aren't covered."

"A mummy case," Pedro cried. "That's it!"

"Why does Old Man Eagle need a mummy case?"

"Does the monster sleep in the mummy case?" ET asked.

"Mummies are dead," Kenny reasoned.

"What about Scooby Doo!" Pedro announced.

"That's a TV cartoon. Tell me again about the monster man."

"It was huge," Pedro explained. "Tall." "Hooded." "Had large hands." "Moved slowly." "And a strange light glowed around it!"

"You didn't have your binoculars?" Kenny asked.

"No," Pedro confessed. "But, I know what I saw." Pedro poked his finger into Kenny's chest,"It...Was...A... Huge...Monster!"

"Cool it!" Kenny responded. "I believe you, but what was it? Big foot? Sasquatch? A marsh man? A man from outer space? CSI team? A bomb squad?" Kenny said rubbing his chin.

"Yeah! You're right. There are a lot of possibilities," Pedro said.

"Do the jugs go in the mummy case?" ET asked.

"Could be," Kenny replied. "Then, what's in the

jugs?"

"The old man's truck isn't around. Let's go in closer," said Pedro, as he bolted forward before anyone could stop him.

Kenny and ET quickly followed. Tall grass, soggy from recent rain, squished under their feet as they darted through the yard to a tall pecan tree. From there, they slinked toward a big white oak tree. The tree's dark shadow shielded them.

Hmmnmmmm

"What's that sound?" asked Pedro.

"A baby crying?" asked ET.

"Hmmm. Hmmm," mimicked Kenny, his eyes searching. "There!" Kenny pointed above Pedro's head. "Bees!" Kenny whispered. Pedro leaned away from a woodpecker's hole, where bees buzzed in and around. "What about the baby?" ET asked. "Shush, ET!" Pedro cried.

"She's right, there's another sound, but it's not a baby. More like a whizzing or whirring noise," said Kenny.

"It's coming from the old garage," Pedro said.

"Why are there green splotches on the walls?" asked ET.

Kenny, checked it out with the binoculars. "It's

moss. Or, old paint splotches."

"Why is the roof crooked?" asked ET.

"The sides are crooked," Kenny answered.

"Why are the sides crooked?" asked ET.

"It's old!" the boys said together.

"Shush, ET! You promised not to ask questions." Pedro reminded her. "Check out the cracks," said Pedro. "Can't see through them. But they're real cool."

"Yeah! Let me see." Pedro took the binoculars and peered through them. "How old do you think the place is?"

"A hundred years?"

"Maybe."

"Ever seen the garage doors open?" asked Kenny.

"Nope. Just the small side door," Pedro answered.

"Why is there a big lock and chain on the garage doors?" asked ET.

"To keep them shut!" Pedro snarled.

"See how the doors and side slant forward." Kenny. "Maybe, shut, the doors help hold the roof up. Open, the roof would fall in."

"Look at the horseshoe," ET pointed her little pink fingernail toward the garage doorway. "Its wobbly and flopped upside down."

"Mom says keep your horseshoes pointed upward

to keep your good luck in," Pedro said.

"The luck's running out of it!" the three echoed.

"This place gives me the creeps," Kenny said with a frown and shook his head.

"Kenny, you go in closer. I'll keep a lookout for you!"

"I don't think so," Kenny said, jamming his hands deep into his pockets.

"What? You scared?" Pedro touted.

Looking down, Kenny scuffed his foot against the tree trunk. "You know I hate being called scared!"

" A smile stretched across Pedro's face. "That's why I said it!"

"Okay,...okay,... Mr. Eagle could be planning trouble. I guess all of us can't go, and you're the best tree climber," Kenny said as he took a deep breath.

"And I have the binoculars," Pedro added.

"You stay here and keep watch," Kenny assigned ET her post, and flicked a stray bee from the top of her hair.

"What's there?" ET asked.

"A bee likes you."

"Eeek!" ET fingered her hair to brush bees from her hair.

"Okay, let's do it, said Pedro. Avoiding the bee's hole, he grabbed hold of the tree trunk and pulled himself up. Soon he was sitting high on a branch. With his binoculars he could see down Eagle's driveway and Eagle Road.

Kenny crept closer to the garage. He stopped at the small entrance and stretched out a hand to grasp

the handle. He tugged. Nothing budged. He tugged harder. Still, nothing budged. "Locked," Kenny whispered.

Err,... Screech,... Err. Echoed from inside.

He went around the side where the mummy case stood beside a small window. He ran his hand over the scratchy surface. "Canvas cover," he whispered. He grasped the thick edge and tugged, but could not move it. Rope tied the canvas on tight. He could hear a faint humming sound coming from underneath. He put his ear against the rough cloth surface. "Hummm," Kenny mimicked.

Err,.. Screech,... Err,... a louder whirling sound echoed from inside the garage.

Kenny took a deep breath, then pulled himself up and stood between a pick and a plow to Iook in the small side window. His hands clung to splintered edges around the window. The window was covered with cobwebs and grime. With one hand, he rubbed a small circle almost clean. Both hands cupped on the sides to stop the glare, he pressed hip face against the cold glass to peek in.

Crash! Thud!

Kenny covered his face as the window shattered around him. The deer horns teetered and flopped lopsided above him. Startled, Kenny leaped from his perch. He turned right, left, and right again searching for who or what did it. He saw Pedro laughing and pointing a bouncing finger at him. "Pedro's rocketing rocks," Kenny grumbled. He'll get us in trouble for sure, thought Kenny. And brushed himself where shattered glass had fallen on him. "Ouch," a piece of glass stuck into his finger. Kenny picked it out and pressed his thumb against the wound. That's what they did on TV to stop bleeding, he thought.

He went to look at the big dark jugs, that sat on a table in the shadow of the garage. He stepped forward, then stopped suddenly. Kenny tried to lift his foot. A dark brown, gooey glob stretched from his shoe to a rock in the ground. "Huh!" Kenny gasped. Next to his foot, in some dirt, was a huge foot print. Big Foot, thought Kenny. He gulped. The Lord will keep me from harm, sprang into his thoughts. His heart raced. We have to stop the old man from hurting anyone, Kenny told himself as he moved to check out the jugs.

Kenny reached out and touched the gooey-brownish stuff coming from one large jug.

Tweet,... Tweet,... Tweet,...

Pedro's warning whistle, thought Kenny. NOT! He's joking again!

"SCRAM!" shouted Pedro. "The old man's coming!"

"Right! Chicken Little!" said Kenny, turning he saw Pedro climbing down from his look-out.

"Scram! Scram!" ET echoes. She jumped up and down and wildly waved her arms.

Kenny stood still and held his breath to listen.

•2•
EYE WITNESS

"He's not kidding," Kenny said, as he whipped the goop from his fingers to his jeans and darted for the tree's cover. Green leaves rustled as Pedro jumped from an oak branch. Kenny put his arm around ET and pulled her close. The three took a deep breath.

They stood still, shielded by the wide trunk.

Rumble, sputter, bang, bang!

A green truck rumbled as it came to Eagle's driveway; it slowed, but passed on by.

"Whew! False Alarm?" Kenny gasped.

"I swear I thought it was Old Man Eagles truck!" assured Pedro.

"We're lucky it's not," ET said, sprawling backward on the grass.

"Well, what did you see?" asked Pedro.

"Tell us, tell us." ET added, as she sat up.

"Not much!" Kenny sighed. "The mummy case has a thick, stiff cloth over it. I thought I heard a humming

sound coming from inside it."

"Is the mummy case a generator, to make electricity?" Pedro asked.

"Could be."

"The baby noise?" asked ET.

"That's coming from inside the garage, but I couldn't see what's making the sound. It was louder after you broke the window!" Kenny glared at Pedro. "You'll get us in trouble!"

"No guts, no glory! And nobody saw us?" said Pedro.

"That's not the point," Kenny grumbled.

"Just keep talking," Pedro said, and resumed peering through the binoculars toward the garage.

Irritated, Kenny continued. "Well, inside the garage was dark, but I could see stuff hanging and boxed piled up everywhere with cob webs and dust covering everything. And when you broke the window, I swear I saw shrunken heads hanging by their hair, but I lost my balance."

"Little heads?" ET said scrunching her head deep between her shoulders.

"Pigmy Heads!" Pedro said.

"That's what they looked like to me," Kenny replied.

"What about the jugs?" asked Pedro. The jugs filled the view in his binoculars. "Looked like they're filled with a dark, mucky stuff," Kenny explained.

"Oil for the old man's truck," Pedro guessed.

"It seemed thicker than oil," Kenny described. "Some of it was liquid with some white stuff globbed together."

Its a brain," Pedro concluded. Peering through the binoculars, he only saw large, dark jugs.

"Yuck!" ET thrust her tongue out the length of her chin.

"You could be right. I saw something on TV where parts of animals were kept in jars with chemicals," said Kenny.

"I heard Old Man Eagle keeps a chicken's foot on a string around his neck." Pedro smiled, and dropped the binoculars to the ground beside him. "Old Man Eagle could be like The Sausage Man that captures dogs and cats and grinds them up into sausage links."

"Like grandma threatens to do with Blondie," Kenny said.

"No !" ET tugged at Kenny's pant leg.

"Near the jugs I stepped in a glob of dark gooey stuff and next to it was a huge foot-print!" Kenny explained, as he whacked his foot where a bee landed on some of the gooey stuff. He scrapped his shoe across the grass to remove the last of the gooey glob. "Pedro, you saw something last night!" Kenny admitted.

"Big Foot!" ET cried.

"I think the old man is up to something," Kenny said.

Rumble, sputter, bang, bang!

A green truck sounded as it turned from Eagle Road onto Eagle's driveway. "It's Old Man Eagle, for real!" Kenny cried.

"Duck!" shouted the three, and dove behind the

trees cover.

Sputter, bang, bang! It clattered as it pulled up the drive and stopped. *Sweek!* Metal rubbed against metal as the door swung open. The springs squawked as Old Man Eagle slowly climbed out. As he stood, he cast a shadow, which stretched the length toward the tree which they hid behind. They heard the rattle of chains and the screech of hinges as the tail gate lowered. They listened to the old man's shuffle back and forth between the truck and garage. *Screech,...clank!* The tail gate closed.

Ken strained to have a glimpse of Old Man Eagle. The old man had thick, silver hair. He was wearing a worn plaid shirt, faded blue-jeans, and a red handkerchief dangled from his back pocket. The shadows of the tree shielded the old man's face

Rumble, bumble, rumble.

Another car pulled up the driveway. It was a midnight black sedan. Kenny shifted, so he could see. The driver's door swung open and a tall man uncurled out. One of his shoulders sat higher than the other and a hunch in his back made him appear shorter than he once was. He wore a grey suit. His belly bulged low. His protruding nose sat above a wispy mustache. Long bony fingers had claw like nails that clenched his clipboard in one hand. The other hand clawed a pencil attached to the clipboard by a long grey string that dangled to the ground like a tail. An oversized black hat shaded his eyes.

He looks like a walking rat, thought Kenny.

Old Man Eagle moved to the black sedan; they didn't shake hands. They moved toward the garage. Old Man Eagle stopped while the man with the clipboard walked slowly around the garage. He look up. He wrote on his clipboard. He looked down. He wrote on his clipboard. He stopped at the broken window. He wrote on his clipboard. The old man moved in the rat-man's shadow. When they got to the doorway, the old man unlatched the chains and dragged it open. The rat man moved inside with his clipboard, but Old Man Eagle stayed outside.

Thud,... thump,.. cluck,...

'What are they doing?" Pedro asked.

Old Man Eagle's head swiveled in their direction.

"Duck!" Pedro whispered as they all hunkered down.

They heard the garage door close and the latch locked. Footsteps came toward them but moved past them.

Kenny cringed. Kenny opened one eye and saw

the man with the clipboard return to his sedan, tipped his hat at Old Man Eagle, and without smiling folded his long body back inside his car.

Rumble, bumble, rumble. The black sedan rolled back down the driveway and drove away.

Thump..., thump..., thump...,

The old man's boots lingered on each step up to the front door of his big house. On the top step, he stopped where a black cat curled, sleeping on the door mat. The old man put out a dark boot and nudged the black curl awake.

"*Mew!*" she cried.

"You good-for-nothing," Kenny heard the old man grumble, as he disappeared behind his door.

"NO!" ET bolted forward.

The boys quickly grabbed her. "What are you doing?" They whispered. "He'll grind the kitty into sausage!" ET cried.

If you get too close, Old Man Eagle will grind you up!" whispered Pedro. If he caught us, who knows what he would do. Lock us in the garage? Torture us?"

"Grid us into sausage," ET quivered.

"Look!" Kenny cried. "Another mummy case," pointing toward the garage, where the old man had placed his load. "What is he up to?" Kenny groaned.

Clunk, Clank, Thud.

The old man's front door opened. "Shush! He's back." whispered Pedro. The three hunkered back down.

Old Man Eagle stood on the porch. In his hand was a long black fireplace poker. Looking around the yard, his gaze landed on the wide white oak tree where they hid. *Thud, Thud, Thud!* His boots echoed on each step. He came toward the white oak, hesitated, and walked right past them. He went to the garage, unlatched the door and, slipped inside. The garage door stayed open.

Kenny's heart was pounding, and he heard ET's knees knocking together!

"Let's go!" Pedro cried.

"Shush, he might hear us," whispered Kenny.

Thud... thump,...cluck,...Whack! Thud! Thud!

"Get back here!" cried the old man. *Crash,... bang,... rattle,... Thud!* "You can't get away!" *Whack! Thud! Thud!* "I'll kill each of you varmints!"

Suddenly the garage was silent. The old man lunged outside the garage, and dragged and relocked the door shut.

The kids watched him plod to the porch with the

fire poker grasped tightly in his hand. Blood clung to it.

"I'm out of here!" Pedro said, leaping up and hitting his head on the bee's hole entrance. "Ouch!" Pedro clutched his head, where a knot began to swell.

"Ouch!" something pierced ET's hand. "Bees!" She pointed toward the bees beginning to flow out of the tree's woodpecker hole.

"Go away!" Pedro tried to sweep the bees aside. "Ouch!" A bee drove its stinger into his other hand.

"Go on now. Get out of here you young-uns!" Old Man Eagle cried.

"Go! Go!" cried Kenny. He grabbed ET's hand and set off, running toward school.

"He'll grind us up!" ET shrieked.

A few bees squished under their moving feet, as the three took off. Several bees trailed after them. Their legs were a blur moving toward school -- across the green meadow, around the still pond, over the broken rail and wire fence, below the one-armed tree stump on the ridge, and down the black-topped road. The boys pant legs and shoes were damp, and ET's dress had a tear. They reached school with two minutes to spare.

Kenny smacked at the bees which still circled them. Wincing, he pulled out two stingers that had found skin. They got me," he said, rubbing the red spots.

"Ouch!" ET flung her arms franticly. "Ouch!" Holding her palm to Kenny, where a bee wiggled and dangled from its stinger. "Me too!" she cried, as tears began to flow.

"Cry-baby. Its just a bee sting," Pedro said.

Kenny grasped her hand and pulled out the stinger. Then he lifted her small palm up and began sucking on the pierced spot and then spit on the ground. "Saw this in a Western." Kenny said, shaking his head back and forth.

You scared?" Pedro asked.

"Never!" Kenny replied. "The Old Man saw us."

"Don't worry. Old people don't remember things very long," Pedro said.

"Hope you're right," Kenny replied.

"Where's your binoculars?" ET asked.

"Oh no!" Pedro cried. "I left them by the big white oak tree! Consider me grounded - unless I come up with a really good story."

Ring..., ring... The school bell rang.

"Let's get going. The last thing I need is to be late and have to go see Mr. Pine, the Principal!" Pedro said.

"Let's take ET to see Nurse Kathy to be safe," Kenny

said, and he led the three to the school's sick room.

"ET will have to stay," said Nurse Kathy.

Kenny looked at ET's palm, it already had a large swollen knot where the bee got her.

" ET. The Lord will keep you from harm," Kenny whispered into ET's ear. "That makes me feel better," Kenny said as he ruffled her hair smiling.

"I was having fun, and I got in the bees way," ET said softly.

"Don't tell anyone," said Pedro as he moved between them.

"See you later, kid," Kenny said. Noticing his top button had come undone, he buttoned it up. Waving behind, he and Pedro darted off to their class.

•3•
AN ASSIGNMENT

Kenny and Pedro arrived in their classroom just as their teacher, Miss Brown, positioned herself by the front bulletin board.

Noise-maker time, Kenny thought as he and Pedro scurried to their seats.

Miss Brown stood shorter than most of the kids even in her high heel shoes. Her long black hair snaked around and down her back. Around her neck hung a knotted lanyard with noise makers dangling: duck-call, kazoo, tuner, whistle. Behind her, Kenny noticed new stuff on the bulletin board.

Twirlll,... Miss Brown's gold whistle shrilled and all went quiet.

"We have a new project," Miss Brown boomed. "A school-wide project."

Kenny saw her arm sweep across the bulletin board's top lettering... P I N G O. Underneath, a gold key was placed on the left side of what looked like blue ocean with waves.

"And you know what that means?" Miss Brown asked.

"Focus time!" Kenny and the class replied. Then, various songs belted out around the room from previous lessons.

"I have just the song," Miss Brown began. "Bingo! Who's sung this before? A couple hands popped up, including Kenny's. Miss Brown moved to lift up a poster board from her desk that had the song spelled out that she wanted the class to sing. "This is not Bingo, but PINGO. Switch a letter, and a word, and the old becomes new," Miss Brown said. Then she raised to her lips the silver tuner from her lanyard and blew.

Humn,…

Miss Brown blew the perfect note as she raised her other hand as a signal to begin singing.

Kenny's eyes met Pedro's who had twisted backwards in his seat and they did what they called a loop-de-loop as their

PINGO

There was a Principle had a goal,
And PINGO was its name-o.
P-I-N-G-O!
P-I-N-G-O!
P-I-N-G-O!
And PINGO was its name-o!

There was a Principle had a goal,
And PINGO was its name-o.
(Clap)-I-N-G-O!
(Clap)-I-N-G-O!
(Clap)-I-N-G-O!
And PINGO was its name-o!

There was a Principle had a goal,
And Pingo was its name-o.
(Clap, Clap)-N-G-O!
(Clap, Clap)-N-G-O!
(Clap, Clap)-N-G-O!
And PINGO was its name-o!

There was a Principle had a goal,
And PINGO was its name-o.
(Clap, clap, clap)-G-O!
(Clap, clap, clap)-G-O!
(Clap, clap, clap)-G-O!
And PINGO was its name-o!

There was a Principle had a goal,
And PINGO was its name-o.
(Clap, clap, clap, clap)-O!
(Clap, clap, clap, clap)-O!
(Clap, clap, clap, clap)-O!
And Pingo was his name-o!
There was a Principle had a goal,
And PINGO was its name-o.

eyes circled up and around in their socket and then belted out the PINGO song, "There was a Principle and he had a goal. And PINGO was its name-o..."

Looking around, Kenny noticed behind him that Johnny sat silent. He doesn't know how to have fun. Kenny smiled and continued singing, but louder and puffed up like a rooster, "And PINGO was its name-o."

"Fantastic!" Miss Brown smiled as she folded her arms and moved to the center of the classroom and waited until everyone's eyes looked at her.

"P... I... N... G... O... stands for Projects In Goals because, every goal has many projects. Like the Principle's new school project," Miss Brown said as she removed the song's poster board and wrote on the board behind it.

Do Something Good For Older Person

"Your project assignment is to do something good for an older person in our community," Miss Brown said. She continued to explain the school-wide project and how the assignment was a little different for each grade. Kindergartners, had to do the least work and sixth graders the most work.

"Using the PINGO steps will help you do a smart project," Miss Brown said as she moved to the bulletin

board and stuck the word **SITUATION** next to the big gold key on the left. "Know the situation." She stopped drawing and moved closer to the students, "How do investigators understand a situation? she asked and folded her arms. Her eyes scanned from one side of the room to the next as she waited.

A hand raised in the back corner. "Yes Olga," Miss Brown said.

"Ask questions," Olga said.

Olga always has an answer, thought Kenny.

"That is right! Investigators ask questions. Questions will help you understand your PINGO project situation" Miss Brown picked up a couple blue markers and drew swirls just above the word situation. "These curls represent the questions that you will ask your older person," Miss Brown said. "You can ask as many questions as you want, but your PINGO paper must include a write up of these interview questions," Miss Brown said.

Kenny wrote down most of what Miss Brown said as he gazed out the class window at a hummingbird that darted up and down. When Kenny heard Miss Brown say something about *cake*, he turned his eyes back to the front of the room.

"You will begin by selecting a person that will be your PINGO project," she held up a yellow hat, that she turned upside-down to use as a basket. It was filled with slips of paper, each with the name and phone number of

SITUATION:
WHY is this person important?

someone in the community.

One by one, Miss Brown passed by a student who selected a piece of paper from the yellow basket to discover their subject.

Pedro, sitting in front of Kenny, drew his paper. "Mr. Hardy at the Hardware store; I bet he practically built the city," Pedro said.

"That's it, Pedro. The first key to this project is to discover what your person has done and is doing," said Miss Brown, smiling.

Pedro sat up in his seat, pleased with the Miss Brown's attention.

The classroom door opened a crack and an Office Assistant peeked her nose in to hold out an arm with a note for someone in the class. Miss Brown took the note.

"Pedro, pick up your things. Your mother is here to take you home," Miss Brown said reading the note. "Something about bee stings."

"Yes, Miss Brown!" Pedro said as he gathered his book-bag. "Got to go bud."

"Hope ET's okay," whispered Kenny as Pedro picked up his things and headed to the door.

"Two names left," said Miss Brown smiling as she held out the yellow basket to Kenny.

Kenny reached into the basket to draw out his bit of paper. He pulled a slip out, but it was stuck to the last one.

"Choose one, and pass the other behind you to Johnny," said Miss Brow   n.

Kenny pulled them apart, placed one on his desk and handed the other to Johnny. His slip of paper dropped to the floor and the top button of his shirt came undone as he stretched to pick it up. He quickly buttoned up his button.

"Who you interviewing?" whispered Johnny.

"Who cares," Kenny replied.   He rubbed his forehead as he thought about the stinger he took from ET's hand.

"I'm to interview Mr. Sosa at the supermarket. The Candy Man!" whispered Johnny. "I'll help him taste test candy!"

Kenny noticed his folded paper on the floor and reached to pick it up. He unfolded and read his paper.

What?

He slumped down, almost out of his seat. The paper fell from his fingers and floated to the floor...

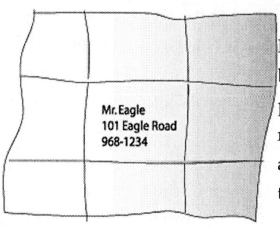

Mr. Eagle
101 Eagle Road
968-1234

Old Man Eagle? Kenny gasped. Can't be, thought Kenny. He picked the paper up and read it, again. Gotta be a different Mr. Eagle, thought Kenny.

"Who did you get?" Johnny peeked over Kenny's shoulder. "Old Man Eagle! I hear Old Man Eagle grinds up trespassers! You scared?" asked Johnny

Of course and you would be too, thought Kenny. "Fear that old man? Never!"

Miss Brown had specific questions to ask the old person during the interviews. She wrote these questions on the blackboard for each student to copy. "Is everyone copying down the questions?" Miss Brown asked, as she wrote the seventh and last question on the board.

"Yes, Miss Brown!" Kenny heard the class say. He sat quiet. He was thinking about Old Man Eagle..., He's the meanest man in town..., He'll grind me into sausage..., He'll store me in a mummy case..., He'll kill me!

Swoosh! A paper airplane flew from behind Kenny and swooped right behind Miss Brown. "Crash and burn!" Johnny whispered into Kenny's ear. "Hey, cute lunch box today, fella,...pink...polka-dots!"

Kenny swiveled in his seat and he and Johnny's eyes met and locked on each other.

Ring....The school bell rang and all eyes sought Miss Brown. She grasped her green duck-call noisemaker from her lanyard.

Quack..., Quack, Quack, Quack..., Quack

"Everything's ducky so go to recess," Miss Brown announced.

And shoes began shuffling out the door.

"Later Johnny," Kenny said swiveling back around as he grabbed his piece of paper and headed to Miss Brown's desk. "Excuse me Miss Brown."

Smack! "Ouch!" Kenny gasped. A paper-wad hit Kenny in the back of the head. Turning, he glared again at Johnny -- he builds the best spit-wads, thought Kenny. It stung where it had hit.

"Johnny come here. Right now!" Miss Brown said, frowning. The two stood at attention in front of Miss Brown's desk. "Yes Kenny?" Miss Brown said, smiling.

"I don't think it's a good idea for me to interview Old Man Eagle... Oops!" His hand swiftly covered his lips, his face felt as hot as a bonfire. "I...mean, Mr. Eagle. Is there somebody else I can interview?"

"scaredy-cat!" Johnny whispered, snickering as he

elbowed Kenny's side.

"Young man!" Miss Brown glared at Johnny. "No more paper airplanes and paper-wads. You get to clean them up as well as any other trash... and then empty the trash-can!"

But... Johnny began.

No buts! Get going. Now!"

"Yes..., Miss Brown," Johnny slowly stooped to pick up the spit-wad that lay at Kenny's feet.

"Kenny," Miss Brown began, her voice barely softened. "I'm glad you got Mr. Eagle; it's funny how fate has a way of stepping in."

Kenny wondered what he had done to deserve the fate of Old Man Eagle – death by grinding.

Miss Brown leaned against her desk, black hair escaped wildly from its clip. "Kenny, I never told you, but I knew your mom in school. She was a grade ahead of me and we always walked to school together. I remember she had a giggle that made everybody else giggle, too. I'm really sorry about what happened to her and your sister," Miss Brown said smiling.

"Thanks for telling me," said Kenny, wondering what else she knew about his mother. Grandma doesn't talk about her much, he thought. When she does, she starts crying.

"I believe your mother would want you to put your whole heart into interviewing Mr. Eagle because she loved to take the short-cut to school across his property. Have you taken it?"

"Not much," Kenny said as he stared at the floor, his head and shoulders slumping forward. Miss Brown had to mention my mother. She doesn't know what they say about Old Man Eagle, Kenny thought. "Yes, Miss Brown." I'm doomed, thought Kenny.

"If that's it, you can go now, Miss Brown said.

Kenny headed for the door, but stopped short. "Johnny!" he said. "Don't miss that one. Kenny pointed toward a paper-wad that Johnny stuck on the ceiling weeks ago.

The rest of the school day was slower than usual because Pedro wasn't around. Kenny's thoughts drifted between his class and Old Man Eagle's mummy cases, dark filled jugs, and strange sounds in the old garage as he walked the long path that circled around Old Man Eagle's property.

ॐ

That night, Kenny lay in bed, awake a long time. Blondie was curled on the floor next to his bed and Kenny had only to lower his hand to stroke her thick, soft fur. He preferred Blondie staying on the floor than messing up his bed. Kenny stared out his window up into the starry sky.

"What do you make of it all, Blondie? The mummy cases? The dark jugs? The big foot print? Old Man Eagle and the fireplace poker? The whizzing sounds coming from the garage? Pedro said he saw a monster in some mist. Remember when my orange kitten disappeared? I blamed you. Sorry girl, I don't blame you anymore. Mr. Eagle probably ground her into sausage or fed her to Big Foot."

The wind whistled through a crack in the window, Kenny placed his hand on Blondie's neck. A lightening bolt dart through the night sky and drive into the ground. A big boom followed. The wind swirled and rain began to hit the ground. A distant window shutter beat like a drum. The roof tops echoed like a cymbal's roll. The wind moaned through the crack in the window.

Interview Old Man Eagle? ...No way! Thought Kenny. He shivered and pulled the covers up around his ears and prayed for a different PINGO person.

•4•
A REQUEST

Kenny woke from a fitful sleep, his legs twisted in the sheets.

"Woof!" Blondie jumped to her feet and licked Kenny's face, her tail flopped back and forth.

"No kisses, girl," Kenny said. "Nightmares, Blondie!" Killer bees were dive-bombing me. I swelled up like a purple grape and couldn't run away from Old Man Eagle's. The old man caught me, rolled me into his garage and ground me up in his sausage machine." Kenny rubbed the red spots where the bees left their marks the day before. He reached and stroked Blondie's silky neck. A drop of drool dribbled from Blondie's tongue onto his bare skin. "Yuck!" he said rubbing off the drool.

Kenny rolled over and grabbed his phone and hit speed dial for Pedro. "I've been calling, and calling!" Kenny said when he heard his friends voice.

"Grounded," Pedro replied.

"Thought so. How's ET?" Kenny asked, holding the phone tighter to his ear.

"ET might be allergic to bee strings, Doc said," said Pedro. "Her one sting is worse than my all of stings. So, she gets to stay home and watch TV!"

"Mine just itched a bunch," Kenny said.

"Same here!"

"What did your Dad say about losing the binoculars?"

"He's furious! Pedro explained. "Things would have been fine, but ET didn't stick to my story."

"Which was?" Kenny asked.

"The bees were in the-one armed tree near the bend in the curve."

In what's left of the tree my mother ran into, Kenny thought.

"He should have believed it." Kenny switched the phone to his other ear.

"Yeah! But Miss Perfect Prince ET mentioned that I lost the binoculars at Old Man Eagle's," Pedro explained. "She also told dad that I broke a window chunking a rock! Now, I'm grounded until I re-pay him for the binoculars and Old Man Eagle for the window.. I'll be gray-haired by then! I'm gonna kill her, if the bee stings don't," Pedro cried.

"How are you going to get that much money?" Kenny asked.

"Oh, mom said I have to earn it by baby-sitting ET and working around the house," said Pedro. "I was also thinking that if I do a good interview, Mr. Hardy might give me a job at the Hardware store to help out!" "Anyway, no more Old Man Eagle's!" said Pedro.

"For you maybe," Kenny said. "Guess who's name I picked out of the basket after you left class?"

"Not Old Man Eagle? You got to be kidding!" Pedro said.

"The one and only. Sneak out and go with me to ask the old man for an interview?" Kenny pleaded with Pedro. "Can't! Mom said, Nada Discoveroso!" Pedro said. "I'm grounded."

"So, your explorer days are over?" Kenny asked.

"Yea, I think I'll be a writer, and I can write about your discoveries!" Pedro answered.

"Start by writing my interview to save me from going face to face with the old man," Kenny begged.

"No way, you're on your own bud. Got to go!"

Kenny put down the phone, picked up his slip of paper and read, for the hundredth time, Mr. Eagle's name. He had done this hundreds of times hoping for a miracle to change the name. When he saw the note still showed Mr. Eagle, he knew he was doomed.

"Maybe it's best Pedro can't come, Blondie. Just in case I chicken out." The Golden Retriever lifted her furry head with a groan. She had curled back to sleep.

You don't just go and interview someone. You have to ask them if they will let you, Kenny's grandmother had instructed. And send a note with the questions on it. And add one asking him why he wouldn't allow a straight road to go through his property, grandmother had nagged.

"Blondie, this assignment stinks. I'm dead if I interview Old Man Eagle. And Miss Brown will kill me if I don't turn in the interview paper. I can't win!" Then some familiar words echoed in his thoughts... "The Lord will keep you from harm." He stopped still and took a deep breath and listened to his thoughts.

"Come on, Blondie. Let's get this over with," Kenny said as he arose, a bit hunched over. With feet dragging, Kenny grabbed his note because he knew it was now or never.

"Woof!" Blondie barked, as they headed out the door. The ground squished under their feet as they walked across Eagle's property. Goosebumps dotted Kenny's arms. Again, the words echoed, The Lord Will Keep you from harm.

Blondie chased after the squirrels. "Woof! Woof!" she chased one up a tree, then another.

"Come here girl, time to quiet down," Kenny called out to Blondie.

Cautiously, Kenny and Blondie approached Old Man Eagle's house. He could see the garage was empty. No mummy cases. No mummy. No jugs. No sounds. No truck. "Don't think anyone's home." Slowly, he approached the front porch. Softly, he stepped up to the door. Gently, he knocked. Nervously, he waited.

Blondie sniffed around the front door. Her tail swished back and forth, which made Kenny feel braver. She'd smell trouble, thought Kenny.

Grass moved at the side of the house.

Growl, Blondie was at Kenny's side. Kenny gulped and held Blondie's collar tight as she pulled against it.

A mangy black cat poked its head around the corner of the house.

"It's just Old Man Eagle's cat, Blondie." Kenny picked up an acorn from a basket of rotting acorn's on the porch and threw it at the cat.

Shoosh! Thud! Meow! The cat flinched when the acorn struck it in the chest, but didn't move.

"Woof!" Blondie barked.

"Stupid cat!" said Kenny, as he watched it wobble

back around the corner. He noticed its bones almost poked through its skin and it struggled to place one foot in front of the other. I didn't realize it was an old cat, and wished I hadn't tossed the acorn now, thought Kenny. "It's best no one's home, Blondie."

Kenny pulled a piece of stained paper out of his pocket. It was the note his grandmother helped him write explaining the class project, and asking Mr. Eagle for an interview. The note was yellowed from much handling in and out of his back pocket. Kenny slipped the note underneath the door.

As Kenny swung around to leave, he found his face smack dab in the weave of old man Eagle's blue jeans. Kenny gasped and stumbled backward a few steps, then froze.

Grrrr,... Blondie crouched next to Kenny -- the old man had caught her off guard too.

Kenny grabbed her collar and pulled her close.

"What do you want?" grumbled the old man. The sun was at his back, outlining his shape and shadowing his face.

'Sir' Kenny replied, the word stuck like gum in Kenny's throat. His palms itched the more he rubbed them on his pants.

"Sir,   .. need an interview... I need a good local

... I... mean, a good grade." The words came out like he had a mouth full of chunky peanut butter. *Grrrr!*

He's not turning Blondie into sausage, thought Kenny. He took a tighter hold of Blondie's collar. "Quiet, girl!"

Old Man Eagle stood still.

Get a hold of yourself, thought Kenny. He took a deep breath, then blurted out his practiced line. "Sir, I have a project to do. I first have to interview my assigned person. I drew your name out of Miss Brown's hat. So, I have to interview you," Kenny said. His body swayed back and forth.

'Oh?' grumbled the old man. He said no more but kept his eyes on Kenny. "I have some questions my teacher, Miss Brown, gave me to ask." Kenny answered, and waited what seemed an eternity. He thought he would work on the interview part and then work on the project part.

"Not today," growled the old man, his voice low and steady. The old man shifted backward, his face remaining in the shadow. "Come back tomorrow afternoon."

"Okay. Thank you, sir," Kenny said, then he jumped off the porch and took off running toward home. "Come on Blondie!"

•5•
AN INTERVIEW

The next day came quickly. I'll skip the interview and make up the answers, Kenny thought, running his hand down Blondie's back. "Would that be cheating Blondie?" Kenny asked.

"Woof!" Blondie's tail beat the floor.

"Guess, I have to do it the right way, Blondie. You'll protect me, won't you girl. Old Man Eagle let me come and go yesterday without harm. Kenny picked up his note pad and pencil and reluctantly headed to Old Man Eagle's.

"Woof!"

Blondie followed Kenny down Eagle's Road and up Old Man Eagle's driveway. Kenny thought it best *not* to use the short-cut to Old Man Eagle's. Blondie, stayed close and, wagged her tail back and forth as they trod down the road. With each step his legs got heavier, and his shoes dragged on the road.

Kenny wished Pedro was with him. He could wait

outside -- just in case something happened. Then again, I might be better off without him, as Kenny thought of the broken garage window. Sometimes Pedro causes trouble. "If the old man got angry, who knows what he would do,...Grind them into sausage?"

Dark clouds began forming and the wind began to blow colder. A distant rumble signaled bad weather coming.

"If I survive this interview, Blondie, maybe I will get a good grade. Maybe the old man will kill me. Maybe, I'll discover the secret hiding in the garage. I'll pretend to be a detective, Kenny thought and somehow this made him felt braver. He took a long deep breath in and slowly blew it out. He stood taller. He buttoned his collar button which had wiggled undone. And then he continued forward with long steps.

Kenny stepped right up to the door.

Knock, knock, knock.

He waited, one foot swiveling back and forth, on its heel. One hand thrust into a pocket. The other clenched his yellow note-pad.

Blondie sniffed the tall weeds beside the steps, squatted and left her scent. Then she came and sniffed along the front door. Blondie would smell danger, thought Kenny. Blondie then plopped herself beside

Kenny. Her long furry tail beat a path back and forth across the porch.

Blondie's ears suddenly pricked up and listened to something he couldn't hear.

"What is it, girl?" asked Kenny. Then, he heard the crunch of gravel under car tires from a car coming down the driveway.

Rumble, bumble, rumble.

A midnight black sedan approached the house. The rat-faced man, thought Kenny. Goosebumps dotted his arms and legs.

A trap, thought Kenny as he heard those familiar words of protection echo in his head, "The Lord will keep you from harm." Kenny looked at Blondie and wished he could use telepathy, mind conversation. We might be in for it, Blondie! A breeze flowed across the back of Kenny's neck, and his shoulders tightened with the coolness.

The car stopped, and the driver's door swung open for the tall man to uncurl out of the car. He held a clipboard. With long bony fingers, he grabbed his black hat and tipped it forward. "Good day," said the man with the clipboard, without smiling.

His hunch seems larger, thought Kenny.

A few large rain drops began to drop from the

dark clouds crowding overhead.

Kenny again hit his fist against the door and waited.

Knock, knock, knock.

Creak.

The door opened. Old Man Eagle towered before him. Kenny wanted to run. He didn't. The old man said nothing, but looked from Kenny to the rat-faced man. Then he stepped forward from the darkness and down the steps and stopped an arms length from the man with the clipboard.

"Done anything about the garage?" rat man asked.

"Not the right time," Old Man Eagle replied.

"Mr. Eagle, the right time may never come and if it does it will be too late."

"Don't worry, I've passed your rules and regulations for years." Old Man Eagle snapped.

Kenny saw the Old Man was mad.

"If that's your decision, then I have no choice but to give you this." His long bony fingers unclipped an envelope from the clipboard and handed it to the old man.

Suddenly, a flash of light brightened the darkening sky. Startled, all three looked toward the sound. Thunder *boomed* from the same direction. Raindrops came down hard and fast.

Grasping his black hat, the rat-faced man tipped it toward the old man. Without smiling he folded his long body back inside his sedan.

Rumble, bumble, rumble. The black sedan rolled away.

Thump..., thump..., thump..., the old man's boots landed on each step. He came up next to Kenny. "Animals stay outside," he grumbled, his shirt was spotted from the rain.

"Yes, sir." Kenny replied. "Stay here, Blondie!" Kenny commanded, pointing next to the front door. He wanted to say, stay alert and be ready to run at a moments notice.

Kenny politely waited for Old Man Eagle to go inside and then followed him in. He blinked several times as his eyes tried to focus when he moved out of the rain, into the darkness.

Old Man Eagle clutched the large envelope the man with the clipboard gave him. He took a letter opener off a table, jabbed it into the envelope, and sliced it open. Sliding the contents out, he stared at some large red letters stamped across the white paper.

Kenny strained to see the big red letters stamped sideways across the paper

C O N D E M N E D. What does it mean? thought Kenny.

Kenny stood still waiting for the old man to say something. Kenny was in the middle of a sitting room. On one side, there were two oversized lounge chairs that looked like a lot of people had sat in them. On the wall behind the chairs, hung a picture of the old man surrounded by smiling kids. He looked at another picture. It was a bearded, Young Man Eagle standing beside a rocky river bed holding a large silver pan in one hand and a golden nugget high in the other. On a small table, between the chairs, sat a model train engine and three attached cars. The mangy, black fur ball of a cat was curled up on the edge of the circular, floor rug. Old Man Eagle's cat is inside, thought Kenny, as he tried to see if Blondie was still by the door.

"Meow!" the black cat cried. It slowly raised its head to see who had arrived, then slowly lowered it back down after it noticed Kenny.

Kenny pulled on a string dangling from his pant leg waiting for the old man's attention.

Finally, the old man placed the letter opener down on a table next to a pair of binoculars.

"First things first," Old Man Eagle said, his voice was husky. "Do you know who these belong to?" He held up the pair of binoculars, the broken leather strap dangled lifeless. "Found them in the yard."

The skin rippled down Kenny's back. Kenny recognized the binoculars. Pedro will be the death of me! Kenny thought.

"No!" Kenny said. His throat was dry. His heart pounded. "Never seen them before." Old people forget things quickly, thought Kenny. The old man can't remember me! Could he? Kenny's eyes and Old Man Eagle's eyes met.

"Guess I was mistaken," grumbled the old man. He placed the binoculars back on a table and stood completely still for what seemed like forever to Kenny. Then Old Man Eagle turned. "Like a biscuit with honey? Sweet-tea?" asked Old Man Eagle. The Old Man Eagle motioned to a tray on the table beneath the front window with a plate of biscuits, a bear with honey, and a pitcher of iced tea. Two napkins, plates, and glasses sat beside them.

Kenny stared at the table. The old man is going to poison me, he thought. Stretching to look out the front window, Kenny saw Blondie lying down on the top step, her tail motionless. Stay put, Blondie, he almost blurted out. He pulled rapidly on a blue string attached to his pants.

"A biscuit, please." Kenny answered with good Southern manners. Kenny's stomach growled as he stuck out an almost-clean hand and took a biscuit. Just past the old man, through the archway in the kitchen, he saw one of those large dark jugs sitting in a window sill. Are the biscuits safe? Kenny wondered.

Kenny waited to take a bite of his biscuit until Old Man Eagle chewed and swallowed his. Then, Kenny wolfed his down. Biscuit with honey… Yumm!

The Old Man poured two glasses of iced tea and went to sit in the blood-red leather chair. He motioned for Kenny to sit down in the tattered yellow-and-black-striped lounge chair.

"Ouch!" cried Kenny, as he jumped back up.

The old man reached over to the chair and pulled out a letter opener. "I was looking for that," said the old man.

Kenny returned to the chair. It's like a bumble bee

-- soft, round, with a stinger, he thought.

Putting aside his biscuit, "Young man, do you have some questions to ask?"

"Yes, sir," Kenny reached into his back pocket and pulled out a pencil and a small yellow notepad. He flipped over the cover, revealing the list of Miss Brown's questions. "I'm suppose to write down what you say -- is that okay?" Kenny asked.

"Sure, it's an interview," Old Man Eagle replied.

Kenny slowly, but precisely, read: "N u m b e r 1: W h a t i s y o u r n a m e ? "

The old man was slow to respond. He seemed preoccupied and kept glancing at the paper with the big red letters. Slowly he said and spelled out the letters of his name.

Kenny wrote in his note pad:

Kenny read the next question: "N u m b e r 2: W h a t i s y o u r b i r t h d a t e a n d t h e p l a c e ? "

Kenny waited. He repeated the question. Finally Old Man Eagle answered.

Kenny wrote:

June 28, 1919
Star City, Arkansas

Kenny read: "Number 3:   Where do you live? Oh, I know the answer to this one."

"Yes," the old man answered.

Kenny wrote:

Rose City Arkansas

Kenny read the next question on his notepad. It was a long one, so he read it a bit louder and slower, in case the old man was hard of hearing:

"Number 4:   When you were ten years old, how much was the cost of an ice cream cone, the cost of candy and the cost to go to the movies?"

"Those things were special. We couldn't afford them like today, but sometimes, if we helped out at the country store, we got our choice of a piece of candy. Movies were a deal, 25 cents for two! And you could stay there all afternoon and watch the same movies over and over," responded the old man.

Kenny wrote:

25# lots of movies

Kenny read: "Number 5: Describe what was important when you were about twelve years old?"

"At your age." Old Man Eagle said and looked down as he scratched his chin. "Well, we didn't have television or computers, and didn't need them. We worked long hours around the family farm. Life was full of adventure. We made our everyday work fun. I was a thief when I stole eggs from the hens in the morning. I was an adventure hunter when I hunted possum for dinner. I was a famous Jockey on a racing stallion when I rode the old mule into town."

"Spent all your time working?" asked Kenny.

"No. I had plenty of free time with my friend Willie Joe. We built a raft and floated down the Arkansas River, built a triple-decker tree-fort, trapped raccoons to make hats with tails, and hunted squirrels to cook over camp fires. "Squirrel Delight is mighty tasty!"

"Squirrel? Yuck!"

"Yep, tastes like chicken," added the old man. "As I grew I helped build things like the garage out back."

"Garage?" Kenny perked up.

"That one." The old man pointed out the window. "It was just a wood shed before 1928. We enlarged it into what it is today. Pop, Willie Joe and I cut the cypress planks for the sides, and pieced together the frame, all in two days. We got cypress planks from small sawmills along the banks of the Arkansas River. The garage used to house a truck *and* equipment and dirt floors were good enough." Old Man Eagle looked toward the paper with the red letters. "Now it barely holds itself up," said the old man. His head lowered with a frown.

"The garage was build for the truck out front?" asked Kenny. He wanted to keep the old man talking about the garage to find out what secrets he kept inside.

"Nope, Pop's old truck."

"Your life sounds like that kid we read about in school, Tom Sawyer," Kenny said.

"Similar time."

A single ray of light slithered through the blinds and into the room, shining on Old Man Eagle's face. The old man continued talking. Kenny stared at the old man and saw the deep grooves outlining his mouth. He noticed the old man's gray blue eyes, his hair of pure white except for a streak of light red above his forehead, and his surprisingly, strong-looking arms. Kenny also noticed that his red shirt was coming un-tucked and, through worn spots, it showed a white T-shirt. The Old Man's shoes were sturdy and almost covered up the fact he was wearing socks of different colors -- one red, one blue. You aren't suppose to mix colors -- it's not right, thought Kenny.

Kenny wrote:

life, like tom Sawyer Kid

Kenny glanced again at the jug in the window, and past it, to the garage. He looked back at the old man, then down at his notes. His hand tugged at a loose yellow thread which dangled from the chair. He drew in a breath. *Hack! Cough! Hack!* The words caught in his throat.

"Tea?" asked the old man.

Kenny nodded yes. The old man grasped the pitcher's handle and filled Kenny's glass, spilling some onto the tray. Kenny grabbed the glass with both hands and guzzled down the sweet tea.

"Now what is the next question?" said the old man.

His eyes met Old Man Eagle's. He swallowed, then reached to pick up his notepad, that had slipped to the floor. He stared at the next question on his yellow notepad. The Big Kahuna question, that should reveal his secret in the garage, thought Kenny. Kenny's fingers found the yellow thread again and tugged.

Kenny sluggishly read: "N u m b e r 6: W h a t f i l l e d u p y o u r d a y s _and_ f i l l s t h e m u p t o d a y l i k e w o r k, h o b b i e s, o r v o l u n t e e r i n g ? "

"Well, that is a good question." a smile curled up on one side of his mouth as he looked out the window and then back at Kenny. The old man took in a full breath of air before speaking, "I retired from working the Railroad Mule Service."

"Mules?" Kenny blurted. He ground up mules in the garage, he thought.

"That's what some people called us, others called us, Superpostmen! Mailmen of the railroads!" added the old man.

Kenny mouthed the word as he wrote:

Train mailman

"That's what they called us. Clerks of the railway mail service. We flipped letters into little boxes in a swaying railroad post office car, going sixty-five miles an hour." The old man continued. "I was responsible for thousands of post offices."

"Wow! You went to all those post offices?" Kenny asked.

"No, only saw their mail," The old man answered. "We helped each city by sorting their mail. We caught their mail while on the railroad. You've seen the movies. A guy on the train wearing a red handkerchief around his neck and thick-rimmed goggles, to protect his eyes,

leans out of the train and grabs the mailpouch. They had a hook to snag the mail bag and pull it in." The old man almost smiled as he moved his hands and arms to show how he reached out from a moving train to grab a strung-up mail pouch. The old man leaned close to Kenny. His voice lowered to a whisper. "If you missed a catch you'd report that it was raining or snowing too hard or that the sun was in your eyes." The old man scrunched his right eye together.

He winked, thought Kenny. He mimicked Old Man Eagle and squeezed his eye together. They told white lies!

The old man traced a weathered but strong finger along the locomotive replica sitting on the table between them. "I picked up, sorted, and delivered the mail on the railway routes belonging to the Cotton Belt: the Chicago, Rock Island and Pacific; the Missouri Pacific; and the Texas and Pacific railroads. I spent over twenty years on the railroads, from 1948 to 1968. Yep, I started with steam engines and ended with locomotives. We griped and groaned when we had to take our examinations and when we had to work holidays like Christmas."

"They made you take tests?"

"Sure! How else would they know you could sort the mail into the right pigeonhole?"

"Pigeons helped you?" Kenny asked.

"No. That's what they called the wall of small boxes we sorted the mail into," replied Old Man Eagle. "A box for each post office."

Kenny wrote:

Cotton Belt Railroad

Maybe the old man stores train engine parts in the mummy cases and engine oil in the jugs, thought Kenny.

"With all the mail I picked up and delivered," began Mr. Eagle, tilting his head to one side, "I never stopped wondering what was in each letter. Bad news? Good news?" "There was one sweet-smelling, pink envelope that was addressed to _me_. The other clerks passed the pink envelope around keeping it just out of my reach and a gust of wind blew it out the back door. I still don't know who sent me _that_ pink letter. There was even a coconut used like a postcard that came from Hawaii. It had a painting of a palm tree with a red and yellow sunset setting over the ocean... it didn't fit into a pigeonhole."

Kenny thought he saw Mr. Eagle smile.

"Back then <u>all</u> mail was important. Too much junk mail these days," he growled. "A waste of everybody's time."

"My grandmother loves junk mail, especially mail-order catalogs," Kenny said. "There isn't a catalog that she hasn't ordered something pink out of." "Clothes. "Shoes." "Furniture." "Food." "Even garden plants."

"Delivered by mail?" Mr. Eagle asked.

"Somebody delivers the stuff to our house. Guess it's the postman," Kenny answered.

"Now your question also asked about hobbies.

"Yes, Sir," Kenny said as he looked down at his notes and noticed that his question sheet had a number seven on it, but had no question next to it. He didn't remember a seventh question. So, thinking he was just about done with the interview, he turned his pencil upside down and erased the number seven.

"When I was young," the old man began, "I wanted to strike it rich and live like a king. Gold! I wanted gold! I thought Mother Earth would show me her golden wealth in the ground. So, I packed up my things and went to California's Gold Country. Got me a pick, a shovel, a pan, and a gold-mining claim in the foothills of the Sierra Nevada Mountains."

Kenny looked out the window toward the garage and visualized a treasure chest of gold hidden behind the walls under the floor.

"Boy, I worked hard," Mr. Eagle said, and sighed, shaking his head side to side. "I discovered lots of speckled gray rocks -- called granite."

"And the gold?" Kenny looked back to the old man, his brows drawing together.

"I found one nugget." The old man reached down his shirt collar and pulled out a large gold nugget, hanging from a cord. Old Man Eagle's fingers stroked the smooth but rippled surface. He picked up the picture next to the bumblebee chair, "That's when I discovered this nugget"!

Kenny wrote in his notepad:

gold panning

"Kids think you wear a chicken's foot around your neck."

"That's for witch doctors and wizards," Mr. Eagle said.

"Some kids think you're one," Kenny added cautiously.

"You don't say. Scared of me I bet?" Mr. Eagle rubbed his chin. "That's just fine. And don't' you go telling them any different. I need my privacy," said Mr. Eagle, pointing a finger at Kenny. Suddenly something caught his attention outside. The old man moved over to the window and peered out. The rain stopped.

Kenny stretched this way and that, to see outside.

Old Man Eagle looked back at Kenny and then moved swiftly to the back door, "Get out! Move along!" he yelled as he went out the door. *Wham!* The back door slammed behind him.

•6•
THE INTRUDER

From Kenny's seat, through the kitchen window, he saw who ran from the property. Pedro. He's going to get us in deep horse-poop, Kenny thought. Maybe I should run out the front door, thought Kenny. Nope, then Old Man Eagle will know I'm with Pedro. I'll pretend I don't know who he ran after.

Kenny's hands shook as he grabbed his pencil and pad and followed Old Man Eagle out the back door. Kenny, went closer to where Old Man Eagle stood in the garage doorway. Kenny noticed the window that Pedro had broken, was patched with screen meshing tacked around the edges. Deer antlers still slumped sideways just above the window.

Mr. Eagle, shook his head side to side with eyebrows draw together. The old man turned around in the doorway. He reached high and unhooked what Kenny now recognized was a heavy rusted chain with a small bear trap on one end. A dead rat dangled from the trap. Blood oozed from the rats body where the trap pierced the fur.

Old Man Eagle held the rat with one hand as he bolted the garage door tightly with the other. "Stinkin rats! I'll mash every one," Old Man Eagle said, scowling. "Lad, do you know who that intruder was?"

"No!" Kenny replied. "I didn't see anyone." His heart jumped up and down and felt like it was going to bust through his skin. His shirt top button popped off as a bead of sweat ran down his neck.

Kenny watched Old Man Eagle grab a shovel which leaned against the garage and drag the rat by the bear trap across the ground to a small clearing in the garden. He dug a small hole, dropped the dead rat into it, and covered the rat with a layer of dirt. "Fertilizer," Old Man Eagle said.

Gulp! Kenny froze, motionless. Fertilizer, he repeated to himself as his arm pits poured out sweat.

Old Man Eagle hung the trap on a nail poking out of the garage and tossed the shovel to one side. Looking around, his gaze rested on a white wooden box which had fallen to the ground. "That boy pushed over the supers and bolted," grumbled the old man pointing to the wooden box and shaking his head.

He called the top to a mummy case a super, thought

Kenny. Still frozen, Kenny, just stood and stared, not sure what to do. Run? Or, help?

The old man bent down and grasped hold of the white box. The muscles in his arms showed. He placed the super on top of a stack of the same kind of boxes. Then he threw a thick white cover over it. He stood up and brushed himself off. "I should have extracted these weeks ago," the old man mumbled as he wiped his forehead and hands off with the red handkerchief from his back pocket.

"Sure," Kenny agreed, not sure what to say. What had the old man not taken out of the mummy case? What had Pedro seen? Kenny stared at a red lady bug crawling on a weed next to the old man's shoe. Mr. Eagle's toe circled, then squashed the bug. That's what the old man could do to me, Kenny thought.

Jerking suddenly as the cell phone in his pocket rang and vibrated. Kenny knew the ring. He didn't move. Then a voice called from the distance, "Ken-n-y! Ken-n-y!"

"That's my grandmother," Kenny said, "she's expecting me to come home.   Sir, thank you for the interview."

"Sure," the old man said. "Best go along while the weather holds."

Kenny thought Mr. Eagle looked like he wanted to talk more, but Kenny wanted to make tracks homeward. "Blondie! Blondie! C'mon girl! Time to go!" Kenny cried.

Blondie poked her head around the corner of the house. "Woof!" Blondie barked, and came running with her tail bouncing back and forth.

Kenny and Blondie took off running down the short-cut toward home. After a safe distance, Kenny turned and craned his neck to snatch a last glance at

Old Man Eagle's place. Dark clouds hovered above it and threatened more rain. A sliver of sunlight hit the garage and cast a long shadow stretching down the pathway toward him. Then Kenny remembered what question _he_ wanted answered-- The GARAGE! "Blondie, the GARAGE! Mr. Eagle said nothing about _the secrets_ inside the garage! I can't believe I didn't ask the right question.

"Woof!" Blondie barked. She squatted by the tall weeds. "Woof!" she barked again.

I'm so lame! I didn't do it right!" Kenny agonized.

Kenny arrived home, dropped his backpack, and ran to his room. He grabbed his cell and hit the speed-dial for Pedro.

"Arf! Arf!" Blondie barked. She sat at his feet, her sides heaving for oxygen.

Pedro picked up on the first ring.

"You almost got us ground into sausage!" cried Kenny. He paused for a deep breath and then continued, "how could you snoop around while I was inside Old Man Eagle's house?" Exhausted, he sprawled out on the bed.

"You're not meat. So, what's the fuss? I thought you'd keep Old Man Eagle occupied?" Pedro replied.

"And I thought you were grounded!"

"The garage was terrible," Pedro announced. "The door was un-locked. It made tons of noise when I opened it. I knew, you'd hear. So, I went in fast. It was so dark I couldn't see. I smacked into something furry and hard dangled from the rafters. It scared me! I flung my arms through a thousand cob webs trying to get the thing out of my face. That's when I screamed and bolted for the door and crashed right into the mummy case. The rest is history," Pedro announced, almost in tears. "A nightmare!"

"It was a rat smashed dead in a bear trap," Kenny said.

Ugh!

Why do you sound funny?" Kenny asked.

"Novocain!" Pedro replied. "Mom took me and ET to the Dentist's. Tongue's still numb!" he mumbled. "That's why Mom gave me the afternoon off."

"Did the dentist use that drill? *Whrillllll...*", Kenny made the sound of the dreaded dentist's drill.

Pedro cringed, "He sure did! Did I ruin your interview? I didn't expect the old man to be watching the yard" he mumbled.

"It's okay, we were finished."

"The mummy case is just a stack of white boxes," Pedro mumbled.

"Yeah, Mr. Eagle called them *supers*. Blow by blow,

Kenny relived his afternoon at Old Man Eagle's."

"Old Man Eagle's not angry?" Pedro mumbled.

"No, but he put a big lock on the garage door," Kenny added.

"What do you make of it?" mumbled Pedro. "Weird. Can't believe the old man said nothing about what he does inside the garage?"

"Gosh, and I can't believe I didn't say the right thing to get him to talking. I thought for sure Miss Brown's questions would trick him into talking about his secrets inside," Kenny explained.

"I'm surprised too. It's not the end of the world. We'll come up with something." Pedro said.

"Guess what the old man has?" Kenny asked.

"I dunno," Pedro responded.

"Your dad's binoculars!"

"No way!" Pedro gasped, not sure if he should be excited or frightened. "Did he remember you?"

"Don't think so," Kenny said fingering where his top shirt button belonged.

"Supper time!" Kenny's grandmother called.

"Got to go, Pedro! Bye."

Before going down to eat, Kenny took out his interview notes and smiled. "I did it. Miss Brown is going to love this," he said with confidence.

•7•
POURED GOLD

Two days passed before Miss Brown returned the graded interview papers. When she did, Kenny was surprised. At the top of his wasn't a big blue A++ but big red letters:

<u>I N C O M P L E T E</u>
W h e r e   i s   t h e   s e v e n t h   q u e s t i o n ?

Miss Brown dismissed the class for the day. Kenny placed his paper inside his binder and placed this in his book bag.

"Kenny, I want to speak with you before you leave," said Miss Brown. "You can't start the next phase of the project assignment without a complete interview and your paper recorded nicely what Mr. Eagle used to do, but there is no mention of what he does these days. It's as if the interview was ended interrupted," Miss Brown observed.

Kenny eyes widened and didn't say a word, but wondered if Miss Brown had talked with Old Man Eagle.

"Your interview paper gets no grade until all seven questions are completed. Do I need to say that you could use a good grade!" Miss Brown explained and gave him one more day to complete the interview.

"Yes, Miss Brown," said Kenny. He wanted to tell her it was all Pedro's fault, but he knew better. And besides, he *had* left off the seventh question which Miss Brown copied for Kenny on his yellow notepad.

Maybe the seventh question will get Old Man Eagle to tell me about the secrets in the garage, thought Kenny. He remembered a TV show where they killed someone who tried to uncover a mystery. And maybe the old man won't tell me, thought Kenny. Big clouds clustered outside. Rain, he thought as he headed out the door to catch up with Pedro who was just outside the classroom.

"Come with me, Pedro, to Mr. Eagle's after school," Kenny pleaded.

"Can't, I'm grounded," said Pedro. "But, if you bring back the binoculars, I think I have enough saved to buy a new window. Then I can be un-grounded," Pedro explained.

"How did you do on your interview paper?"

"I got a C. What is there to say about Mr. Hardy – he likes to build things and help people buy paint, lumber and nails,...End of story. Miss Brown said I needed more information," Pedro explained.

"I thought you would get an A for all of the pictures in it," Kenny added.

"Miss Brown said I had too many." Pedro stood with hands on hips to mimic and repeat Miss Brown's words, "Pictures enhance words not replace words. Guess I'm not cut out to be a writer."

Kenny watched Pedro join ET in the pick-up circle as their mother drove up. Kenny turned and headed toward Mr. Eagle's.

Kenny went down the black-top and stopped at the bend in the road, below the one-arm tree stump on the ridge. He tried to remember the last time he saw his mother and sister. Staring at the stump which marked the accident's spot, it looked like a cross to him. Bee's started gathering. *Buzz...*, *Buzz...*, *Buzz...*, Kenny continued on, swiftly dodging the active bees, across the broken rail and wire fence, around the still pond, and across the green meadow to Old Man Eagle's house.

Looks quiet. But Old Man Eagle's green truck is here. He must be around. Kenny thought about running home to fetch Blondie when he went up to the front door. _Knock. Knock._ No answer. Impatiently, he waited. I'll go to the back door, thought Kenny. Following the house around, he found the back door. _Knock! Knock! Knock!_ Again, no answer. _Err..., Screech..., Err...,_ Kenny heard a familiar whirling moan. He turned toward the old garage. His eye noticed the broken window. A strange golden light was glowing from inside. And a weird mist was pouring out the garage's small open doorway. _Err..., Screech..., Err...,_ The sound continued. Fear drew him toward it. Sausage grinding machine? Kitten crying? Train engine? He stepped closer, but stopped dead and froze.

An enormous man-like shape stood, just inside the doorway. The monster! thought Kenny. Space alien? Ghost? Robot? Murderer? It seemed a long time before either moved.

The shape moved into the daylight. Arms reached hands high and grasped both sides of his head. Hands tugged once, twice, three times. . . he pulled his head _off._ It was only a yellow hood with a thick veil, thought Kenny.

"Hey, young Kenny. How are you today?" Old Man Eagle said with a grin.

Kenny gulped. "Huh?" Still motionless, Kenny

returned a stiff smile.

Old Man Eagle placed his hood on the ground and tugged at his fingertips to release thick leather gloves covering both hands. Then he ducked back into the darkness of the garage. Then the old man came back into the sunlight, he had removed the large suit he was wearing. In each hand he held large, dark brown, jugs.

Kenny watched every move the old man made.

"What are you up to?" asked the old man.

"I . . . didn't complete my interview. I didn't know about the last question. Miss Brown told me to complete it today," he answered.

"Figured as much. The interview got cut short. Today's fine, if we can do it while I work." The old man walked toward Kenny. *Shwoosh. Thud.* He swung the jugs forward. They landed upright on the grass. The old man stood up straight. Grabbing the red handkerchief from his jean pocket he wiped his brow. "If you remember, I was fixing to tell you about what I do these days when our interview was ended by the intruder in the garage; so, I was expecting you to return... And, you say you left off a question?" said Old Man Eagle.

"Yes, Sir," Kenny said.

Err..., Screech..., Err...

Kenny stared toward the sounds coming from the

garage. "I. . .was supposed to ask you," he began, then reached for his yellow notepad and flipped over the cover where Miss Brown had written what Kenny had failed to copy and she added a bit more. Kenny handed the note to the old man with fixed eyes on the garage.

The old man read the note from Miss Brown:

Question #7
What projects do you need help with?

Help Kenny make a list of projects that when completed will be helpful to you. Kenny will pick at least one project from the list that is:
* Important to you
* Can be completed in a weekend

Mr. Eagle pulled at his ear-lobe, "Project?"

"Miss Brown said projects solve problems," Kenny said as he heard whirling sounds coming from the garage. That sounds like a big problem, he thought.

"Don't know about problems," said Mr. Eagle as he handed the pad back to Kenny and looked at the jugs on the ground, but I know where I was yesterday when we were interrupted. I told you about my younger days

looking of gold and delivering mail. I began to tell you how I struck it rich _not_ in gold nuggets, but in _liquid gold_," said Mr. Eagle.

"Liquid Gold," Kenny repeated, and he remembered the old man's search for wealth.

"That's right . . ._honey!_" said Mr. Eagle. "I struck it rich with honey, from my beehives."

"What?"

"Mind you, I've never made millions but, bees and honey enriched my life beyond my wildest dreams... honey is my hidden gold!

"Honey has been important for a long time." Mr. Eagle pointed to the jugs.

"Honey?" Kenny's eyes grew wide. He went closer and with his finger, he swirled a bit that oozed out from the lid. He smelled it, but there wasn't a smell. His tongue stretched out and touched the gooey stuff. It's sweet! He stuck his finger into his mouth and licked it clean. "It's honey, sure enough!" cried Kenny.

"The richest around," said Mr. Eagle, smiling proudly. "Sunshine makes it extra rich. My secret ingredient."

Kenny picked up the jug. He struggled with its weight, holding it high enough to catch the sunlight. Through its golden color, he examined the honeycomb floating inside. He chuckled, "It's not a brain."

Kenny picked up his yellow pad, which had fallen, and wrote:

"Follow me," Mr. Eagle said, as he went over to one of the tall mummy cases, untied the rope, and pulled off the cover. White boxes were stacked one on top of the other. "Covering the supers keeps the bees from taking their honey back before I can take the honey out," Mr. Eagle explained.

"Okay!" Kenny said. He ran his hand across the heavy tarp and along the stack of boxes. The old man works with honey; who would have guessed, he thought.

"These supers are full of honey and I was fixing to rob them," said Mr. Eagle. "You'd call this a beehive?" asked Mr. Eagle.

"Yeah!" Kenny answered? He had never seen one before.

"These are only part of a beehive. And they're full of honey, just waiting for us to rob them." Mr. Eagle's face looked like a kid planning to steal from a cookie jar.

"Rob a super, is that a project?" Kenny asked poised to write on his notepad.

"Nah, just a days work," Mr. Eagle explained and continued, "When you rob a beehive, you are just removing a _super_! You see, many frames hang in a super, in which the bees build honeycomb from frame edge to edge and then fill with honey."

"What do bees do with honey?" Kenny asked.

"Honey is their winter food source," Mr. Eagle explained. "But they make more than they need. So, I remove the supers they don't need. Then I remove the honey from the frames and replace the empty frames back into the super. I put the supers back on the beehive for the bees to refill with more honey. Then, I rob them again!" Mr. Eagle said with a grin.

Kenny wrote:

Bee frames have honey
frames in super

"If a super is only part, what else makes up a beehive?" asked Kenny, as he slid his hand along the smooth white surface of several boxes.

"Add a base, a large brood chamber where all the bees live, a screen, and a few supers." Mr. Eagle said patting the sides of the white, stacked boxes. "Add a top. Poof!" Mr. Eagle's arms raised high, like a magician. "You have a beehive."

Kenny wrote:

"I can't small talk when there's work to do," Mr. Eagle said as he motioned for Kenny to follow him into the garage.

•8•
ROBBER'S TOOLS

Kenny stepped inside, behind Mr. Eagle. Kenny's eyes took a moment to adjust to the dim light. I'm inside the garage, thought Kenny. *Err..., Screech..., Err..., Whirrr..., Whizzz...*

Kenny looked around and found the noise maker -- in one corner was a large silver cylinder, sitting on a wooden stand, placed on the garage's dirt floor. An electric motor spun something round and round, metal squealed against metal as it turned. That sound isn't a baby crying. But what is the machine for? thought Kenny.

He looked all around. No ground-up animals! Things hung, dangled, laid everywhere – boxes, buckets, hoses, tools, siding, signs, wire. Cobwebs stretched across every corner and he caught sight of a rat running the length of a rafter. He frowned. Piles of problems; or, a room with things to discover, Kenny thought. Kenny and Mr. Eagle's eyes met.

"This place holds a lot of useful stuff," said Mr. Eagle. Mr. Eagle walked to a white box and slapped the side. "This is a Brood Chamber," he said, and slapped another white box, "and so is this."

"They all look the same," said Kenny.

"The brood chamber looks like a big super. But to the bee, they are very different," said Mr. Eagle. "A hundred thousand bees can live in a Brood Chamber."

"A hundred thousand bees are in there!" Kenny stepped backward and looked around searching for diving bees.

"Not in these. They're empty," Mr. Eagle assured him. He pulled out a pamphlet from underneath some tools and blew the dust off it. "Here take this!" he said shoving the small paperback pages in Kenny's hands.

"Beekeeping," Kenny read. He flipped the pages and stopped on a picture of three bees. "w o r k e r, q u e e n, d r o n e," he read. "This is great. Thanks." Kenny flipped through the rest of it. Lots of words, not many pictures, he thought. He rolled it and slipped it snug in his back pocket.

"Have you been stung by a bee?" asked Kenny

"Lots of times. When you've been stung as many times as I have, you almost get immune to it," Mr. Eagle said with a smile.

"Don't think I'd like that," said Kenny. "Did you get stung a lot when you were a kid?" asked Kenny.

"Sure did! As a boy I never had special clothing with elastic closures, like now. And, when I helped I seemed to rile up the bees. So, bees came after me like dive bombers. Usually, they can't penetrate clothing. One bee, however, would always be determined to sting me, and that bee would work to find an opening in my clothing. Once, a bee snuck all the way up my pant leg, then worked up to my waist; but, before a stinger found skin, I unzipped my pants and was able to wiggle the bee out. I've always been good at avoiding stings, but if I did get stung, I knew a secret way of handling bee stings," said Mr. Eagle.

"What's the secret?" asked Kenny.

"Spit on it!" said Mr. Eagle. "Other people go to

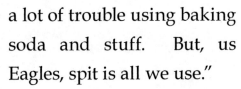

a lot of trouble using baking soda and stuff. But, us Eagles, spit is all we use."

"Really! Would spit help someone who might be allergic to bee stings?" Kenny began, "My friend Pedro's little sister, ET, might be allergic to bee stings."

"Now that's a different ball of wax. Bee stings are very dangerous for those who *are* allergic to them. They need more than spit," warned Mr. Eagle.

How many beehives do you have?"

Mr. Eagle counted on his fingers, "Somewhere between 24-35."

"Thousands of stingers!" Kenny shivered.

"All those bees will mind their own business if not disturbed," said Mr. Eagle, he looked stern. "If they sting, it's to protect their food. Honeybees work hard and don't give honey away. That's why we have to *rob* their beehives."

"Won't they attack you?" asked Kenny.

"Not after we use a smoke screen," said Mr. Eagle.

"Does the smoke get into their eyes, so they can't see you robbing them?"

"No. They think something is on fire. They forget about protecting the honey and begin protecting their queen and their hive," said Mr. Eagle.

"Are they called supers because they're super full of honey?" asked Kenny.

"Good enough of a reason." Mr. Eagle patted the boy's shoulder. "Let me show you more." He went over to the work table.

Rattle, clank, clink.

The old man shuffled things aside. Something across the garage caught his eye, and he walked over and lifted it off a rusty nail. "Here's something, all

beekeeper's use -- the hive tool."

"Looks like a crowbar," Kenny observed.

"Yes, but hand-sized. This helps me pry up beehive tops and honeycomb frames.

Clank, clink, rattle.

Mr. Eagle put the hive tool aside and, shuffled things aside on the workbench. He stopped and pulled the red plaid handkerchief from his back pocket and

wiped his brow. "Ah!" Then he quickly stepped through the small doorway. Kenny began to follow after, but his foot caught on a hard edge. Kenny tumbled forward and into Mr. Eagle's arms.

"Watch yourself, young man!" Mr. Eagle helped Kenny to his feet. He had slipped on some thick, brown leather gloves. "Beekeeper's gloves," said Mr. Eagle. He smiled as he stretched his hands forward and turned them to display both sides.

"Ah! You found it." Mr. Eagle cried, as he reached down for the object that had tripped Kenny. "My smoker! If I burn a coil of cardboard inside and squeeze the bellows to force air out, smoke blows out of the spout. This is what I use to make the smoke that quiets the bees so I can open the hive."

Mr. Eagle's other hand held a large yellow hood he had brought from outside. "This is a beekeeper's hood. The veil and screen protects the face and eyes from the bees." He pointed toward a peg in one corner. "I'm trying to do things right. So, I got this new beekeepers suit that I'm suppose to wear when the bees are mad," he continued. "I've worn it only one other time and I moved like cold molasses. Darn thing's so thick and heavy! I never need one in the past, but the inspector has new rules I'm suppose to follow."

Inspector, Kenny thought, must be a friend of Mr. Eagles. Smoke? It is the *weird mist* surrounding the garage. It must have been Mr. Eagle's smoke quieting bees and the monster in the mist was just Mr. Eagle wearing his suit, hood, and gloves. And the golden glow was light passing through honey jars. And the gooey glob I stepped in was honey, Kenny determined. Boy will Pedro be surprised when I tell him, Kenny

thought.

"That's all you need to work with bees and beehives," said Mr. Eagle.

Kenny pulled out his notepad and wrote:

beekeeper tools: hivetool, smoker, gloves, hat

"You need bees too!" Kenny added.

"You are right. Have you seen my beehives?" Mr. Eagle asked, he smiled and looked into Kenny's eyes.

Kenny drew backward, "No. . .where are they?"

"They're in a good spot, but I don't want young'uns messin with them. Angry bees stop making honey or swarm to different locations," cautioned Mr. Eagle.

"I would never do anything mean to your bees," Kenny said, wondering where the bee hives were.

"Like those in the big tree's woodpecker hole?" asked Kenny.

"Nope, that's a new swarm with a new young queen, looking for a hive to call home -- I'm getting a hive ready to move them into," said Mr. Eagle.

"Moving a swarm is that a project I can help you with?" asked Kenny.

"Don't think so, just another day's work for a beekeeper," said Mr. Eagle.

"This was all my pop's stuff, his tools, and his bee hives." Mr. Eagle's eyes looked around at the things in the garage.

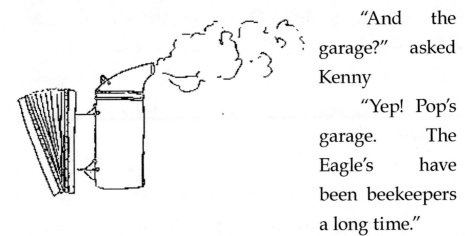

"And the garage?" asked Kenny

"Yep! Pop's garage. The Eagle's have been beekeepers a long time."

Kenny's eyes followed Mr. Eagle's as he saw a rat scurry across the floor. Mr. Eagle picked up a long stick. "_Shush,_" Mr. Eagle put a finger to his lips.

Whack!…Whack!…Whack!

"Darn Varmints, I'll kill every one. Got away," Mr. Eagle said, setting the stick aside.

"Rats! Now, that has got to be a problem?" asked Kenny. "I can help you get ride of rats." Kenny poised to write this in his notepad.

"Na, I've got a bear trap that takes care of rats."

"Grandmother says that mice, spiders, and rats don't like order in a room. I'm good at straightening things, if you want, I can clean-up the garage as

my project and it might help keep the rats away?" asked Kenny.

"Not needed," Mr. Eagle replied. "Everything is where I can find it! Besides, I might have to tear the garage down."

"Why?"

"Some say the garage isn't good enough anymore, and that it is gonna fall in on me" Mr. Eagle said as his brows scrunched together and his lips pressed downward. "They don't understand that cypress planks last forever!"

•9•
STOLEN GOLD

The old man waved a hand for Kenny to follow him. "Time to work!" Together, they carried one of the supers inside the garage.

"When the supers are full of honey, like these, they are really heavy. But with your help, they are light as a feather." Using the hive tool, Mr. Eagle pried off the super's top. "It's fitted with hanging frames." He pried out a frame, then held it out for Kenny to observe.

"Where is the honey?" Kenny asked. He saw white waxy stuff filling the frame.

"You'll see." Mr. Eagle walked over to a wooden bin, already full of beeswax bits. "My de-capping bin," he said, reaching for a worn but sharp knife. "The bees fill the frame with honeycomb, then the bees fill each wax-cell with honey, and then they top each honey-filled cell with a wax cap."

Kenny leaned close and watched Mr. Eagle prop up the frame.

"To rob the honey, we have to cut off the wax tops," said Mr. Eagle as his knife sliced back and forth across and down the length of one side and then he turned the frame to the other side and sliced down the length cutting off the caps as wax caps slithered, folded, and flopped down into the bin below.

"The honey isn't coming out." Kenny stretched his neck closer and examined the frame.

"That's why we do the next step," Mr. Eagle explained. He walked over to the corner and placed the de-capped frame into the large silver cylinder.

"Looks like a huge tin can on a wooden stand with a can opener attached to one side," said Kenny. So, the noise maker is used for honey and not for grinding up animals and making sausage, Kenny chuckled to himself.

"It might at that, but it's *my* honey spinner." Mr. Eagle took out the red handkerchief from his back pocket and gently wiped a cobweb attached from the ceiling to the dulled silver surface. "This silver lady has helped me extract a lot of honey by spinning the honey from the frames. At one time, she was the biggest and fastest around."

Kenny watched their reflections move along the spinner's dull metal surface. The old man looks like a tall skinny clown.

"She holds four frames. Some spinners these days hold many more frames," said Mr. Eagle. He took another frame and began to de-cap the honey-filled cells. "Take this." Mr. Eagle stuck out his knife. It held some oozing honeycomb.

Kenny stepped backward. "No thank you." His mouth squeezed shut, remembering the bitter, slimy, squash his grandmother forced him to eat last week.

"Honeycomb! Take it. You know you want to." Mr. Eagle nudged Kenny, "Chew it like gum."

Mr. Eagle reached out and grabbed a sample of bee's wax drenched in honey. He placed it into his mouth.

Kenny then did the same. He reached out, pulled off a bit of honeycomb and slipped it into his mouth. "It's sweet and chewy!"

After the sweetness was gone, _Splutt!_ Mr. Eagle spit the remaining bee's wax on the ground and pinched off another oozing hunk of honeycomb.

Splutt! Kenny did likewise. "Tastes better than gold!" said Kenny.

"I'll second that," said Mr. Eagle. Their eyes met for a moment.

After four frames were de-capped and placed in

the extractor, Mr. Eagle set the motor in motion.

Err,... Screech,... Err,...

The silver cylinder echoed, bounding back and forth between the boards as it swirled. Honey spun from the cells, ran down the inside of the cylinder and began to flow out of a small spigot into a clean white bucket.

"Too cool!" cried Kenny.

After a bit, Mr. Eagle stopped the spinner, turned the frames over, and began the motor again.

Err,... Screech,... Err,...

Honey continued to flow from the spigot. When all the honey was spun from the cells, the de-honeyed frames were returned to the super. "I'll replace these into the hives next spring and the bees will repair the wax cells, and fill them with honey again," said Mr. Eagle.

"Then we rob them?" Kenny asked.

"Yep, you got it." Mr. Eagle repeated this cycle, with Kenny's assistance, all afternoon until all the outside supers were emptied of their golden treasure.

Kenny wrote in his pad:

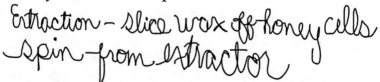

Extraction – slice wax off honey cells
spin from extractor

Kenny watched the honey slowly creep up the white bucket's side. "Almost full," announced Kenny when it came close to the top. Mr. Eagle replaced the full bucket with an empty white bucket.

Mr. Eagle was silent and Kenny grew uncomfortable. Finally the old man spoke. "I had someone break that window pane over yonder, a while back. I got it patched up with wire screen right now," Mr. Eagle said in an even tone. "Know who did it?"

Kenny stood still. For a moment, their eyes met. Kenny felt his cheeks pulse red hot. Mr. Eagle didn't see it was me and Pedro, thought Kenny. Or did he?

"This shed is private property," Mr. Eagle continued. "I have equipment I could never afford to replace."

"N... no.... I... don't know who did it," Kenny said, his eyes stayed focused on the dirt floor and a bead of sweat trickled down his back. Pedro's trouble, thought Kenny.

"Hum." Mr. Eagle looked away and said no more.

They worked together in silence. Kenny continued to take the frames in and out of the super to help Mr. Eagle.

Mr. Eagle stood up holding two frames. "See how

these honey filled wax chambers bulge with honey," he held out one frame. "See how these others don't bulge."

"Why is that?"

"Younger and stronger bees fill the chambers with more honey because they work better and get sick less."

"Isn't a bee just a bee?"

"No. Younger and stronger queen bees, produce healthier, stronger bees. My queen bees might be a bit older, but their bees know how to make the best honey. But the stronger bees often go to hives with weaker bees and steal honey.

"Robber bees? No way!"

"Do sick bees produce sick honey?"

"No. Sick bees can't work as hard and produce smaller amounts of honey. Commercial honeybee hives, replace their queens yearly with young queens. So their bees are strong and produce more honey. I'm sure some of them are robbing honey from my beehives."

"Why would bees steal honey?" Kenny asked.

"Because it's easier than making it."

"Aren't you a commercial beekeeper?"

"What I mean is they have a lot more hives than I do, and they are in it to make as much money as they can," Mr. Eagle explained. "Your help is making this much easier. Wish you had been around to help last year when I couldn't complete the extraction season."

"What stopped you?"

"Well, I was careless and stumbled over a sheet of tin and fell hard into an active bee hive. They got riled up a bit. I was stung by a mean bunch of bees. Seems my skin isn't as thick as it once was. Also, I twisted my ankle in the fall and combined with the stings, it sent me to bed for awhile."

"Were they killer bees?"

"Na. Just worker bees protecting their honey. I was in the middle of moving some hives from one location to another. They get a bit testy in moves, so I cover them up to make them think it's night time and add some smoke to keep them quiet.

"Their stingers went through your beekeeper's suit?" Kenny questioned, his eyes wide with curiosity.

"Well now, I wasn't wearing the suit, just the hood. My kids got after me because I wasn't wearing a suit. At that time, I didn't own one and didn't think I needed one. So, my kids got me that suit," Mr. Eagle explained, pointing toward the beekeeper suit he had placed on the wall peg."

"So what did you do?" Kenny asked.

"It was awhile before I had enough strength to work. Couldn't finish extracting the honey. Winter came quickly and made the honey was cold and thick to spin from the frames. It was this spring by the time I completed extracting honey from those hives."

"Don't you mean, robbing honey?" Kenny asked.

"Yes, robbing honey from the hives!" Mr. Eagle laughed.

"Why is the beekeeper's suit on the peg right now?"

"And not on me?" Mr. Eagle said finishing Kenny's sentence. "There are no bees in these boxes. I'll do it right next time I'm moving the bees, just in case they get riled up again."

"What do you do with all of your honey?" Kenny asked.

"I eat a lot of it. My kids and grandchildren eat a lot. My friends use a lot. And I donate the rest." Mr. Eagle stopped, stood up straight, and stared forward.

Kenny noticed Mr. Eagle seemed like he went into a trance as he spoke. "My father started donating honey to the white steeple church down the street. Pop always said, God's will was sweet, like honey. He also said, that in Bible days, land with honeybees was considered a gift from heaven, because honey was a liquid gold to

Kings. He also liked to quote the Bible: _My son, eat thou honey, because it is good; and the honeycomb, which is sweet to thy taste. Proverbs 24:13"_

Kenny watched Mr. Eagle as he stood motionless with a faint smile.

"God provides the honey. So, I do like my dad. I donate honey to the church and they sell it to raise money for the poor," Mr. Eagle said, coming out of his trance with a twinkle in his eyes and a big smile. "Did you say Miss Brown wants to know about hobbies and volunteer work?" Mr. Eagle suddenly said.

"Yes," replied Kenny.

"Think honey donations count as volunteer work?"

"I'd say so." And Kenny wrote in his notepad:

"Does the tall man, who drives the dark black car and carries a clipboard, buy a lot of honey?" asked Kenny.

"I wish he was buying honey," Mr. Eagle sighed.

•10•
LIFE DOESN'T SEEM FAIR

"The man with the clipboard is the county Health Inspector who is trying to *force* me to stop giving it to the church to sell."

"He can't do that! Can he?" asked Kenny.

"Rules have changed. What was okay once now isn't okay," Mr. Eagle grumbled.

"Doesn't seem fair," Kenny said.

"Life isn't always fair," said Mr. Eagle.

Kenny thought of his mother and sister and the accident.

"Rules for processing honey have changed over the years that the Eagles have been beekeepers. Once, this garage was the best around for processing honey. Now, the Health Inspector says I must have scrub-able floors, walls, ceiling and two metal sinks with flowing hot water." Mr. Eagle said, looking from one rough wall, to the beamed ceiling, to the dirt floor. "This will never meet the Inspector's rules," said Mr. Eagle, shaking his head back and forth frowning. His shoulders slumped forward. "Might be time to change some things."

"Use your house!" Kenny blurted, thinking he solved the problem.

"Good thought. The rules say food processing must be in a space separate from a home's main kitchen -- and the separate area must be clean and tidy."

Kenny looked around at the piles of tools, cans, boxes, boards and dangling cords. I could help him with neat and tidy, but that won't change the surface of the garage's walls, thought Kenny.

"The Health Inspector, gave me two weeks to make this garage meet the codes."

"Can you do it?" asked Kenny.

"Too difficult" Mr. Eagle answered, shaking his head slowly back and forth.

"How about tricking him?" Kenny said as the old man and his eyes met.

"Trick's and lies eventually trip *you* up," said Mr. Eagle holding eye contact with Kenny.

"But, what are you going to do," said Kenny looking downward searching his thoughts for the right thing to do.

Mr. Eagle looked around from one tool to the next. "The Eagle family has processed honey the same way for a long time. The Inspector doesn't understand that the bees and god make the honey. I just put it in jars!"

"How about building a *new* place to meet the codes?" asked Kenny. "Maybe we can work on it for my class project?"

"Not the right time. There's a time and season for everything. Time for building up, time for tearing down," said Mr. Eagle.

"This isn't so hard, I can help you with it."

Mr. Eagle and Kenny's eyes met and they smiled as Mr. Eagle reached a hand out and ruffled the top of Kenny's hair.

Clang, rattle, bang, bang, sounds rumbled outside.

Mr. Eagle dropped everything and stepped through the doorway to investigate. Kenny was right behind him. Pedro laid on the ground, sprawled out between the pick and plow.

"You okay, lad?" Mr. Eagle helped Pedro to his feet.

"Pedro, what are you doing?" Kenny cried.

"I was just walking by and saw you in the garage an..." Pedro said, brushing off dirt, quickly trying to think up a believable story.

"How'd you know where I was?" whispered Kenny into Pedro's ear.

Mr. Eagle was busy returning the pick and plow to their spots leaning against the garage.

"Your Grandmother," Pedro whispered in reply.

"Would you like to look around?" Mr. Eagle winked at Kenny.

"Sure!" Pedro answered.

Kenny quickly took Pedro into the garage and showed him around. He showed him the tools and explained how to rob honey from bee hives. "Stolen gold," Kenny said, smiling as he showed Pedro the buckets of golden honey.

"What's left to do?" Kenny asked.

"Well, I have to heat the honey to prevent it from crystallizing into sugar and this helps the honey flow through the filter that catches any bits of wax and impurities," said Mr. Eagle.

"Like bee wings and stingers?" Pedro asked.

"And beeswax. Then we pour the honey into jars and jugs."

Kenny pulled out his yellow notepad. He wrote:

put honey in jars

"Can we do it now?" asked Kenny.

"That's another days work."

Mr. Eagle pulled out four jars of honey from a brown

cardboard box. "These are for you and Miss Brown. And this last jar, I want you to deliver for me?"

"Sure! Who to?" Kenny and Pedro both echoed.

"Mrs. Pine is feeling poorly from allergies and she is out of honey," Mr. Eagle announced. "Take this to her son, Mr. Pine, the Principal at your school."

"Piney Principal? Give him honey?" Pedro and Kenny echoed.

"For his mother. She lives with him and his family. If it's too much trouble, I can take it myself."

"Sure, we'll do it. Just give the jar to Mr. Pine, for his mother? Right!" The last thing we want to do is go to the Principal's office, thought Kenny.

"That's it."

"If she's ill, how does honey help?" Pedro asked.

"Something like fighting fire with fire. Since honey contains the pollen that makes people sneeze and cough, it helps people build a resistance to the pollen.

Bees baffle scientists. Honey has so many nutrients, that scientists have tried to create honey without honeybees, but can't. Only honeybees make honey. It's amazing how honeybees collect pollen from all over town, and then return to their hives to make honey from it."

"Magic! Honeybees use magic," Kenny reasoned.

"Maybe they do," said Mr. Eagle.

"Thanks for the honey!" cried Kenny and Pedro.

"My own gold." Kenny announced.

"My own magic!" Pedro announced. "Maybe I'll be a Magician?"

"Magician?" Kenny asked.

"Why not!" Mr. Eagle added.

"Why not!" They agreed, and the three walked outside.

Wham, bang, clunk.

The old man swung the door shut and locked the latch. "It was good to have your help, thanks," he said.

The sun began to set. Grandmother would be calling Kenny inside for supper soon. The boys headed home on the familiar short cut. As they passed through the yard, Kenny noticed that the grass had grown tall and the garden was full of weeds. Even the big white oak had a broken branch dangling dangerously toward the ground. Mr. Eagle could use some help, Kenny thought. Maybe I can list the garden or yard work as a project for Miss Brown?

They stopped a short distance away and looked back. Mr. Eagle's garage was bathed in the fading light of the evening sun. The garage looked different to him now, thought Kenny. He knew the secrets it contained.

"I knew there wasn't mummy cases or bottled brains," Pedro announced.

"I was sure wrong about Mr. Eagle. I thought he ground up animals like the sausage man," Kenny added.

"You're right, he isn't so scary," said Pedro.

"Mr. Eagle is okay," Kenny added. "Glad you came by, Pedro. How's that sister of yours?"

"Nothing wrong with ET! She's been pestering me. So, mom un-grounded me for the day. Mom told me to get lost and find Kenny!"

&

Dinner was just being placed onto the table as Kenny entered the house. "Smells good. Grilled cheese?" asked Kenny.

Blondie ran and jumped up on Kenny almost knocking him over. "Did you miss me girl!" He wrapped an arm around her collar and squeezed tightly.

"I got this in the mail today," said grandmother. She stood to pick up her latest mail delivered trinkets. "Grilled sandwich presses. Kenny, don't you just love them!" she cried. "Yours is the snowflake and mine is a rose," grandmother said as she held up square iron press, the size of a slice of bread rotating to display each for Kenny's approval.

"Cool!" said Kenny. Sandwich smashers, he thought, as he inspected his flattened grilled cheese sandwich. "Grandmother, It's amazing what you get through mail delivery," Kenny said, thinking of the deliveries that seemed to come daily to their doorsteps.

"Look what I got from Mr. Eagle? Honey!" Kenny said. Blondie's tongue licked the side of the jar. "Find some honey, girl?"

"That good for nothing man at the bend!" grandmother exclaimed.

"Not so, grandmother," Kenny said. He saw her eyebrows raise high as he told her all about extracting honey from bee hives. "They look like hives, but they are really brood chambers and supers," Kenny explained. He pulled the bee book from his pocket Mr. Eagle had given him and flipped through it. "Grandmother, do you think if I helped Mr. Eagle around his yard he would give me a bee hive?"

"Might be easier to get a bee hive through a mail-order catalog," grandmother said, never raising her head from the mail-order shoe catalog.

"You can't get bees through the mail."

"Then how do you get them?" grandmother

asked.

"I don't know. Maybe you catch a swarm of them in a tree?"

"What does that pamphlet Mr. Eagle gave you say?"

"I dunno, too many words to read."

"I see," grandmother said reaching for the pamphlet and flipping the pages.

Kenny noticed she looked at the few pictures and stopped to read something that caught her attention. "Hum," grandmother said and she circled something on the pamphlet's back cover. Then she looked up and smiled.

"Your collar button is undone, Kenny."

"It's more comfortable this way."

"Maybe your neck is growing," grandmother determined.

"Maybe," Kenny agreed. "What do you think of this girl?" Kenny lifted a tidbit of his cheese sandwich above Blondie's nose. That was the signal for her right paw to raise to shake, hand to paw.

Blondie's tail flopped back and forth.

After dinner, Kenny stayed up late working to complete the paper on his interview with Mr. Eagle. He stared at the seventh question for a long while.

What   projects   do   you   need   help
with?

Mr. Eagle thinks there aren't any problems, thought
Kenny. Kenny saw many projects around Mr. Eagle's.
"Guess I'll have to fill in the seventh question myself,"
Kenny said as he began a list.

Potential Projects

✮ save garage from rats

✮ help to bottle honey

✮ make yard
    neat and tidy

When Kenny finished typing and printing his
paper he gently put it in his book bag.

Kenny stared out his bedroom window up into the
clear dark sky and focused on one bright star as he turned
off his bedroom light and crawled into bed. Another star

sailed in an arch across the sky and dissolved. "Come up, Blondie! Up girl! Onto the bed, girl!" Kenny said as he tugged at Blondie's collar until she put one paw, then another until all four paws were on the bed and made herself comfortable. All night Kenny and Blondie slept quietly curled next to each other on the bed.

•11•
GOLD STAR PROJECTS

Kenny barreled through the school office door in the morning before heading to class, and found Mr. Pine inside leaning against the front counter. "Oh," Mr. Pine," said Kenny as Pedro smacked into his backside.

"Good morning boys" said Mr. Pine.

"Good morning, Sir," Kenny said as he took a step forward and stretched out his hand with a pink rose covered bag. "Honey. For your mother," Kenny said. His face turned pink as he fumbled with his top shirt button, "We were asked to bring you this."

"We helped jar it!" Pedro added then turned and bee-lined off to class. "See ya at class, Kenny!"

"*You* jarred the honey?" Mr. Pine asked as his left eyebrow raised an inch.

"Yeah,...I mean, yes Sir, here's the note from Mr. Eagle. Actually, we extracted honey from some frames," Kenny added.

"I see. Thank you, Kenny," said Mr. Pine as he

opened the note-card to read.

"Can't be late to class," Kenny backed out of the office door to follow after Pedro.

In his classroom, Kenny grinned as he placed his now-completed interview paper in the assignment bin on Miss Brown's desk. The rest of the school day was like any other day that was until after the last break.

Ring..., Ring..., Ring...,

The bell rang to signal the end of the break.

Miss Brown sat on the edge of her desk next to the now empty assignment bin as Kenny and the other students entered the classroom. Kenny's eyes scrunched together as he recognized the large rectangular pink bakery-box. Someone's birthday cake, thought Kenny. Other students smiled and perked up as they noticed the large pink box too. Kenny's stomach rumbled as his lunch didn't last long. He remembered the candy he saved for his walk home.

Students took their seats.

As Kenny took his seat, he saw the PINGO bulletin board had a second gold key. The key was placed on the right side and the label beside it read - GOAL.

Miss Brown selected a noise-maker from her neck's lanyard and blew.

Whirl..., Whirl,...Whirl...,

"I have a problem," Miss Brown said as she unfolded the sides to the large pink box to reveal the cake inside. She tilted the cake so everyone could see.

Kenny shuffled sideways in his seat to see the cakes white icing decorated with small red pots of gold coins. The pots were evenly spaced.

"My problem is that I have a cake that is too large for me to finish by myself," Miss Brown said.

"I'll eat it, Miss Brown!" Big Belly Billy offered.

"Right! We'll be all over you, like flies on fly paper," Pedro said.

"It will fit in your stomach but will it fit in your mouth" Johnny said stretching out his hand that held a paper airplane and swished it in a circle once and crashed it into his desktop. The boys exchanged green-eyed glares.

"Thank you Billy. That is one plan that would solve my problem to get rid of the cake. What might go wrong with that plan?"

"Billy could get sick to his stomach and throw up," Pedro said.

"Possibly," Miss Brown said.

"No one else would get any," Olga Olive said.

"That's true," Miss Brown began. "What plan do you think might be the smartest way to get rid of this

cake?"

"Cut the cake up for everyone," several students rang out together.

"Yes! And that is exactly what we will do," said Miss Brown.

"Come and get some cake!" Miss Brown said and began cutting the cake into equal sized squares. Students shuffled up for their piece of cake. Each piece had icing with a pot of gold coins. Everyone had their fill of cake and little remained.

Miss Brown walked over to the PINGO bulletin board. "The second key to putting your project into go, is to have a

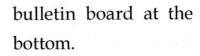

smart goal. A goal that is divided into bite-sized pieces." She said as she pointed to the second key and label, and then she placed a red pot filled with gold coins above the key. "A goal with doable pieces of work,"

"Is that all a smart goal is?" Kenny asked. He liked to do things right, but was that right, he thought.

"Good question," Miss Brown began.   "Billy. Would eating a whole cake be a smart goal?"

"Yes ma'am!" Billy replied gleaming and shaking his head up and down.

Miss Brown smiled back at Billy and moved to her desk to pick a picture and add it onto the PINGO

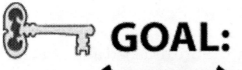

bulletin board at the bottom.

A shark, thought Kenny.

"Do sharks kill everyone that goes into the water?" Miss

Brown asked.

"No," Johnny said. "Usually they just bite off an arm or leg or foot when they are hungry."

"Maybe Billy can eat the whole cake. And maybe he can't without getting sick," Miss Brown began. "Like sharks in the ocean, you work to avoid them and most people do."

"Class, was dividing the cake into pieces a smart goal?" Miss Brown asked.

"Yes!" Several students echoed.

"So, a smart goal *is* done right?" Kenny asked.

"A goal is an end you aim for, Miss Brown said."

"A smart goal is an end aimed for with the situation understood," said Miss Brown.

"Smart goals also can be divided into pieces. Like, the school community project is divided into PINGO people pieces. The big cake was divided into individual cake pieces. And the work you will do for your older person will be divided into a weekend piece." Miss Brown said.

"All the interview papers are finished and graded," Miss Brown said as she pulled the pile of interview papers from her desk and began returning them. "I was delighted to learn about your PINGO person's lives --store owner, weather person, Rail-way postman!" said

Miss Brown.

"Turn to the seventh question in your interview papers. Here you listed some projects to help your older person," Miss Brown said. "Like your piece of cake, you ate a piece that was a smart size. Tonight's homework," Miss Brown began, "Consider your PINGO person's situation that you discovered while spending time with them. Select from the list the work you will do for your older person over one weekend and about eight hours. Choose a smart goal," said Miss Brown. She wrote on the board the homework.

HOMEWORK:

Write down the pieces of work you will do for your

smart goal?

Kenny's brow became hot and damp as he thought about the projects that he had listed on his paper. I don't have any projects, and Mr. Eagle doesn't need or want my help, thought Kenny.

Miss Brown placed Kenny's interview paper on top of his desk. Kenny quickly noticed that Miss Brown had written a great big blue A+.

"Outstanding," Miss Brown whispered in Kenny's ear.

Kenny's eyes looked at the best grade he had ever

received.

"Bet you made up the answers," Johnny nudged from behind.

Turning, Kenny sneered at Johnny. "Watch it. Old Man Eagle taught me how to cast Wizards spells. He said I can use his garage anytime to brew up spells. Toss in a rat, cup of honey, mixed in the spinner with the right words. *Voila!* You'll be in love with ugly Olga Olive and leaving me alone," Kenny whispered with crooked smile.

Johnny folded his arms and slumped down in his seat.

Kenny copied the assignment down and began shoving his things in his book bag when he saw Miss Brown grasp the familiar duck-call noise-maker from her lanyard.

Quack..., Quack, Quack, Quack..., Quack

"Everything's ducky and its time to go," Miss Brown announced.

"I'm out of here," Kenny said as he headed for the door.

Things aren't so ducky, because I made up the list, thought Kenny. He headed out the door.

"I love a brain on a sugar rush," Pedro said as he grabbed another piece of cake and snaked out of the

classroom.

"Miss Brown could have just asked, How do you eat an elephant?" Pedro said when he caught up to Kenny.

Kenny stopped and stared at Pedro. "How *do* you eat an elephant?" Kenny asked.

"One bite at a time," Pedro said and laughed.

Ha..., Ha..., Ha...,

"Going to be a comedian?" Kenny asked.

"Been thinking about it," Pedro replied.

Kenny and Pedro set out to find Mr. Eagle's beehives which they found not too far off the Eagle short-cut home, up the far ridge, behind the one-armed tree stump, not far from where his mom ran off the road.

"We have to treat the bees and hives with respect!" said Kenny. "They have important work to do." He didn't let Pedro get too close.

Pedro's cell sang out a familiar battle cry. "Dad," said Pedro as he pressed the receive button. "Yes, Sir! Kenny and I are working on a class project," Pedro said and rolled his eyes upward and around. "But,...but,..."

Kenny knew that meant *Pedro's* in for it,...again.

"Dad rolls out punishment like toilet paper," Pedro said as he pressed his call end button.

"What's up?" Kenny asked.

"Got to go. I'll call you later," Pedro yelled out as he dashed homeward.

Kenny leaned against the stump and watched Pedro move out of sight as he tried not to think back to the night he lost his family...the heeby geebys rippled through him as well as the familiar phrase, *The Lord will keep you from harm...* he thought on this as a bee landed on his pants knee, moved around as if trying to say something to him and then took flight. Kenny gathered his book bag and plodded downhill toward Mr. Eagle's to deliver Miss Brown's thank you note, and talk about selecting a project.

•12•
BAG OF CHOCOLATE

Clouds gathered and darkened the sky. A cold breeze made Kenny stop and pull his back pack close to his side.

A strange dark cloud in the distance caught Kenny's attention. Long and narrow, it spiraled from the ground skyward. A shiver traveled down Kenny's back and made his heart beat faster, and his feet moved faster along the path.

Kenny arrived at Mr. Eagle's and saw the black cloud was billowing up from a burning pit to the side of the garage. Mr. Eagle stood at the far edge and poked the burning rubble. He recognized a letter and envelop that was singed at the edge of the fire pit. Turning his head sideways and he read, CONDEMNED.

Mr. Eagle never looked up as Kenny approached. "It's a beekeeper's responsibility to maintain healthy bees and beekeeping equipment," Mr. Eagle said. The old man turned his face and stepped away from the smoke. He coughed to clear his lungs. "The hives and gear have foulbrood disease. Have to be destroyed."

"Does it mean the honey is poisonous?" asked Kenny.

"Heaven's no! Bad for bees. With the disease, bees produce less honey. It weakens bees. Slowly the hive dies. I've been rasslin and rasslin, afraid of doing the right thing. Afraid of _not_ doing the right thing. Truth is, I knew what to do. I didn't do it. Things got worse because I didn't do the right thing sooner. Today, I realized I had to do my part. Let God take care of what comes next," Mr. Eagle said.

"Is that being bigger than your fear?" Kenny asked. "That's what Grandmothers tells me to do."

"I reckon it is."

"So what are you trying to say?" asked Kenny, shrugging his shoulders. He watched the red and yellow flames dance with wicked energy.

"Everything has to be burned. Buried. Destroyed," Mr. Eagle replied, his shoulders lowered.

Kenny watched Mr. Eagle drag over a chair and slump in it. Mr. Eagle's hold on the poker loosened and it dropped to the ground. Kenny realized Mr. Eagle had tears in his eyes.

Looking away from the blaze, Kenny spotted the

silver honey spinner dumped by the road for the trash collectors to pick up. His heart began to pound faster and faster as he realized that the flames were consuming frames of honeycomb, beehives, and their honey.

Suddenly, a flame ignited inside of Kenny. "No! There must be something we can do! We can fix it!" Kenny cried. He scooped up a handful of dirt and flung it at the flames. For a second the flames crackled, hesitated, then leaped higher as if Kenny fed them food. "Water!" Kenny cried. He ran to a nearby hose, grabbed the end, and began pulling it toward the flames.

"Hold on! It's too late." Mr. Eagle was just behind Kenny and took the hose from Kenny's hands.

"You're not doing anything to stop the flames?" Kenny pleaded.

"The foulbrood disease has been in the bee hives too long. I should have taken care of things when I first suspected it. It's my fault. I didn't do the right thing," explained Mr. Eagle.

"What do you mean?" asked Kenny, tears filling up in his eyes.

"I could have examined the bees and hives closer, not mixed diseased supers with good ones, bought new queens, and disinfected my equipment. As the inspector said, 'Keep a clean and tidy operation,' Mr. Eagle said as each word came out hard and both hands were firmly on Kenny's shoulders.

"Neat and tidy?" Kenny said, disbelieving what Mr. Eagle was telling him and shaking his head back and forth. "I'm good at that!" Kenny ran to the garage. Quickly, he gathered up several cloths draping over nails on the wall and rapidly smoothed them flat and placed them, one on top the other, onto the work bench. He grabbed an empty coffee can and began picking up tools and jamming them inside. He spotted a fat rat crawling above him across a beam. He reached for a long pole, and began swinging wildly at the creature.

Thud,... thump,... cluck,... Whack! Thud! Thud! "I'll get you!" Kenny's voice bellowed. _Crash,... bang,... rattle,... Thud!_ "You're not getting away!" _Whack! Thud! Thud! Whack! Whack! Whack!_ Suddenly, sounds crackled around Kenny.

Crack, Creek, one ceiling plank of the garage shifted loose and fell.

Boom,...

Dust fanned out as Kenny was knocked to the ground and stuff flew around him.

"Kenny!" Mr. Eagle cried from outside the garage.

Mr. Eagle came into the garage and saw Kenny hunched on the floor. "The Lord will keep you from all harm," Mr. Eagle declared, as he reached his arms around Kenny. "You okay boy?" Mr. Eagle asked.

"What did you say?" asked Kenny, a bit dazed.

"The Lord will keep you from all harm, he will watch over your life. Psalm 121:7" said Mr. Eagle. "When in trouble, I declare the Lord's presence so I know I'll get it." He knelt beside Kenny and helped him sit up.

"You were there,...at the accident ," Kenny said, he rubbed a spot on his head which already had a bump growing.

"Yes. I was the first one there," Mr. Eagle answered.

"Ouch! My ankle," cried Kenny, his voice quivered, but he held back his tears.

Mr. Eagle grabbed a nearby stool and shuffled the stuff on top aside. "Sit down! Let me have a look at your ankle."

Kenny did as he was told and sat on the stool.

Mr. Eagle pulled the red handkerchief from his back pocket. "Wrap this around that cut." Then he stooped and examined Kenny's ankle. He pressed a couple spots. "hurt?"

"Nope."

"How about this?" Mr. Eagle asked, as he rotated the foot right and then left. Kenny winced, then relaxed.

"I felt something pop inside."

"Nothing seems broken, just a wobbly bone. Try and stand on it," Mr. Eagle said, moving to get out of Kenny's path.

Kenny stood and took a forward step. "Yes sir, it's okay."

Mr. Eagle looked around the garage. "That pine support gave way. The cypress beam planks are strong, it's the other supports that can't handle aging. I need to add a couple nails and replace that old plank with a cypress support and she'll be as good as new. Cypress wood lasts forever," Mr. Eagle said inspecting the other boards and beams.

Mr. Eagle stood still and stared downward as if remembering the past. "I was the first one to arrive at the accident. I was finishing up a long day working on the bee hives near the old oak tree, the day was cold, dark, and stormy. The sound of the car hitting and-downing the old oak tree was like nothing I had ever heard. Your mother's car was in flames by the time I reached it. I ran to the car and found that you were the only one alive. I barely had time to pull you out. Then an explosion engulfed the whole vehicle."

"Gas tank exploded." Kenny remembered the reports. Nothing was ever said about Mr. Eagle's help, thought Kenny.

"I stayed until the authorities arrived and they took you to the hospital," Mr. Eagle said. "Nothing more than that. Anyone would have done it," he added.

"I'm glad you found me. Thanks."

Mr. Eagle and Kenny quietly nodded their heads and exchanged a smile.

"I got it!" Kenny pointed to the floor where a dead rat lay under wooden rod.

"That you did. Now we best get outside while the garage is still standing." They moved back toward the blaze, which had begun to lower its flames. Heat from the fire was weakening.

"Wait here." Kenny retrieved his book bag and drew out a bag of chocolates. "I saved them from lunch." They sat down and shared a bag of smooth, brightly-colored balls of candy-coated chocolates.

"Here's a blue one," Kenny said, handing Mr. Eagle a chocolate. "They're lucky!"

"I appreciate that. Guess I need all the luck I can get," said Mr. Eagle.

"Why didn't you tell me that you were at the accident?" Kenny asked.

"Guess it wasn't the right time."

"Grandmother told me that you stopped the county

from building a straight road through your property and that my mother and sister would be alive if there had been a straight road," Kenny said, without looking at Mr. Eagle.

"Fact is, I let the county officials decide which to build -- a straight or curved road. I pointed out, to them, that a straight road would create a drag strip right in front of your school. Curves slow cars down. A straight road would have gone right through the protected marshland as well as my largest set of bee hives."

Mother was traveling real fast, Kenny remembered. A warm glow beamed within him. mom and sis, I love you and miss you, he thought as he looked skyward. A fresh breath filled his lungs and popped his top button open. He left his shirt unbuttoned.

"You're right." Kenny reached in his pack, and drew out his interview paper and the note from Miss Brown. Handing them to Mr. Eagle. Kenny rubbed his hand along the side of his pants leg. Then he reached forward with his hand. "Sir, I came today to thank you for helping me."

Mr. Eagle took hold of Kenny's hand. Like men, they shook hands. "If my memories and my honey were of help, I'm pleased," Mr. Eagle said, flipping through Kenny's paper. "My, this is fancy work!"

"The computer did all the hard work. I just pushed the keys and clicked a few buttons.

"You have a computer at home?" Mr. Eagle asked.

"Doesn't everyone?" Kenny asked. "Grandmother got ours from a catalogue." Pedro helped me put in the bee and flower clip-art. Pedro wants to be a computer artist, " Kenny explained.

"Things sure have changed since I went to school! This looks more like a college paper," Mr. Eagle told Kenny as he grabbed the iron poker and poked the now smoldering fire.

Snap, Crackle, Pop, a flame leaped up as the coals were turned.

"I think my ankle's fine now," Kenny told Mr. Eagle as he unwrapped the red handkerchief.

"Glad to help." Mr. Eagle replaced the handkerchief back into the faded jean pocket.

"I have to pick a _project_ to do for you over a weekend," Kenny said as he plopped the last candy circle onto his tongue. "Something important to you, and not just a days work. You can read what I thought you would want under the seventh question."

•13•
LUCK IS LOOKING UP

"K - E - N - N - Y!   K - E - N - N - Y!" A voice faintly called from the distance.

"Your grandmother?" Mr. Eagle asked.

"No, not grandmother," Kenny answered.

They looked in the direction of the sound, but were blinded by the sun light reflecting off the garage's tin roof and couldn't tell who was approaching.

"K - E - N - N - Y!   K - E - N - N - Y!" the call came again, louder.

As they came closer Kenny saw Pedro pulling a large red wagon. ET carried a box and Blondie was circling them chasing squirrels. "Blondie, here girl!" Kenny called and waved his arms for her to notice.

"Woof! Woof!" Blondie barked, but continued pestering the squirrels.

"Pedro! ET! What are you up to?" Kenny asked.

"Your grandmother thought you would be here and asked us to take this stuff to you." Pedro told Kenny as he strained to pull Kenny's wagon across the grass.

""Why didn't you call?" Kenny said.

"Can't. Dad took my cell away because he didn't like how I did the yard work," Pedro said as he continued to tell Kenny about the hedge he shaped into a mouse head.

"What's in those huge packages in my wagon?" Kenny asked.

"I thought you knew!" Pedro cried. "Your grandmother said it came special delivery from the mailman today. One medium-sized box and this enormous one. It took me, ET, and your grandmother to lift it into the wagon. And, now you don't want it!" Pedro cried.

"Didn't say I didn't want it, just don't know what it is!"

"I know what's inside this box," ET said with a snicker. She plopped her cardboard box onto the ground at Mr. Eagle's feet.

"Is this the young lady who was kissed by the bees?" Mr. Eagle began.

"I'm not allergic to bee kisses!" said ET. Shyly she twisted a bit or pink cloth from her blouse around a finger.

"I'm glad to hear that. Bee stings are very dangerous

for those who are allergic to them," Mr. Eagle said as he gently patted her small blond head.

"Too many bees stung her for her size," Pedro added.

"Kissed me!" ET corrected. "Mom heard you had trouble with mice and said you might want this." ET flopped down and unfolded the flaps to one box. Blondie came and sniffed the box ET carried. "_Woof!_"

"Go on, Blondie. Go get the squirrels!" Kenny pulled his dog away. An orange and white furry head peeked out. "_Meow! Meow!_" the kitten cried. "I named her Meow because she is always talking."

"_Meow! Meow!_" Meow cried.

"She's from a long line of mousers," Pedro added.

"I could sure use help with those varmints," Mr. Eagle said as he stooped down and ran his large rough hand down the kittens back almost flattening it.

Mr. Eagle looked up toward the porch to see that old Blackie had come to the edge. "Blackie will welcome _Meow's_ help with varmint catching duties. Tell your mother, thank you."

"_Meow! Meow!_" the kitten cried and jumped from the box and began nosing its way toward the garage.

"See! She knows where to go get them!" cried ET.

"Is that the chicken foot around your neck?" ET asked pointing her pink finger nail to the old man's neck.

"Young lady, this is a gold nugget," said Mr. Eagle as he pulled out the golden stone and held it closer for ET to see.

Kenny noticed Pedro and ET looking at the garage where the roof line slumped. "I knocked a beam down," Kenny explained.

"Seems I have two choices for your weekend project, Kenny," Mr. Eagle began, "Either fix the garage or tear it down."

"This will help you fix the window." Pedro pulled out a heavy brown wrapped package for Mr. Eagle from the wagon. "It was kind of an accident."

"I tied the bow," ET added. A pink hair ribbon was tied in a bow around it.

Mr. Eagle took the package, removed the "wrapping and ribbon. "A window pane?" Mr. asked.

I'm awfully sorry, sir," Pedro said as he scuffed a foot along the ground, his head lowered, his shoulders slumped. "I threw a rock too hard and it broke your garage window."

Mr. Eagle smiled, "I accept your apologies." Then Mr. Eagle turned and looked at Kenny, "Do you have some crow to eat?"

"Yes, Sir. I knew who broke your window and who those binoculars belonged to. I was too scared to admit it. *You* knew all along?" Kenny asked.

"I had a hankering you were hiding something," Mr. Eagle began, "A lie can easily catch up with you and bite you. With the truth out in the open and with this window, we can fix the damage. Pedro, let's go put it in. And Kenny why don't you get the binoculars from inside."

"Yes, Sir!" Kenny dashed toward the door. He found the binoculars sitting right where he last saw them. Then he dashed back outside.

"Here you go Pedro!" Kenny said.

"Dad will sure be glad to see these." Pedro placed them with the boxes in the wagon. "Mr. Hardy at the Hardware store said he knew the window's size," Pedro explained.

"Let's see," Mr. Eagle said and moved to the window and removed the old wire mesh and broken weathered window pane. Positioning and tapping the new pane into place, he secured it with a couple nails and placed sealant around the edges to finish it off. "There, good as new!"

"Why didn't you fix the window before now?" ET

asked.

"Just wasn't the right time!" Mr. Eagle replied.

"It's time for something else." Pedro grabbed a couple crates beside the garage and positioned them in the doorway, picking up a hammer from inside the garage, he reached his hands up high for the horseshoe. Pedro twisted the horseshoe around, with the arms pointing upward, *Whack!*, he tightened the nail. "Your luck was running out!" Pedro announced. "If you ever need more help, I'm your man." He said hopping off the crates.

"My luck is indeed looking up. I feel as happy as a dog with two tails," said Mr. Eagle, a big smile reached across his face.

"Grrr-woof! Woof!" Blondie barked, nuzzled, sniffed and pawed at the biggest box in the wagon.

Mr. Eagle began studying the labels on the containers which the wagon carried. Thorn Company starter kit, he read, "Shush! Listen!" Mr. Eagle placed his finger to his mouth.

Buzz..., Buzz..

"Buzzing?" Kenny said. He put his ear to the package.

Mr. Eagle opened up the packing paper which was taped to the side in a plastic envelope. He unfolded the paper and read the list of the big box's contents, "Beginner Beekeeper Starter Kit: complete hive, bee book, smoker, hat, veil, gloves, hive tool, three pound package of bees, and one queen," Mr. Eagle read, and he smiled. "Your grandmother ordered this from a bee supply house and a mail man delivered it? Postmen today are amazing!"

ET's eyes got big. "Bees? I don't want to get kissed by any bees again."

"We won't let them," Mr. Eagle assured.

Kenny came closer to read the label and wrapping paper.

"Grandmother said you could order anything through the mail.

Rumble, bumble, rumble.

A car was coming down Mr. Eagle's driveway.

"Its tires rolled over the gravel and came to a stop. A door squeaked open and shut, and foot steps crunched as they came around the house.

Rat-faced man, thought Kenny as he, Pedro, and ET eye's met with brows lifted high.

"Saw the smoke from the road" the man's long bony fingers clenched a clipboard and a black hat balanced on top of his head.

"I thought the Health Inspector might poke

around," Mr. Eagle said. He began jabbing at the remaining humps of ash. No flames danced.

"I'm just doing my job," said the man with the clipboard. He stepped toward to the garage and noticed the slumping roofline.

"The garage is no concern of yours anymore. If you check out this fire pit, you'll see, I'm officially out of the beekeeping business. I'll be selling no more honey." Mr. Eagle announced.

The man with the clipboard stood still and looked at Mr. Eagle. Then he turned his head to stare at Kenny, Pedro, and ET. "There are specific rules that must be followed if anyone wants to *sell* any kind of food."

"And, rest assured," said Mr. Eagle, "If we *sell* any food stuff, or give it away to sell, we will first contact you to find out the latest dos and don'ts, since they seem to change over the years," Mr. Eagle winked at Kenny.

The man with the clipboard moved closer to the boxes on the wagon. He looked the boxes up and down, and his nostrils flared as he smelled the air. "Just doing my job," said the man with the clipboard. His long bony fingers pulled the piece of paper from his clipboard and holding it up high ripped it right down the middle. "Don't guess I need this any more," he said while tossing the pieces of paper in to the soldering ashes, the white

paper turned to black as it burned.

Mr. Eagle, Kenny, Pedro, and ET eyes widened as they looked from one another to the blackening pieces of paper.

The man with the clipboard looked back to the garage. "The hardware store just got a fresh shipment of cypress planks that might help fix that roofline." Then he turned and went back around the house.

Rumble, bumble, rumble. The midnight black sedan was heard leaving. "You didn't say anything about *my* hive in the wagon?" asked Kenny.

"It wasn't the right time."

"Can I fix up the garage for my class project?" asked Kenny.

"I reckon, it is time to give her a face-lift," Mr. Eagle agreed. "Why don't you boys go bring in that old honey spinner from off the curve? We can disinfect her, rebuild her engine, replace her belt, and build her a new stand," Mr. Eagle said, smiling as he pointed to the curb where the spinner had been placed. "You'll need the silver lady for your honey!"

"Guess it's time for me to be a bee keeper," Kenny said putting his ear closer to hear the sounds as he stroked his hand across the box of bees. "I'll keep my bee hives neat and tidy!" announced Kenny.

"Can I help?" Pedro asked. "I want to be a beekeeper too."

"Only if you do it right!" Kenny announced.

"This will help you seek the right way," Mr. Eagle said as he placed the gold nugguet around Kenny's neck. "When you go to sell your honey, you can check with Mr. Health Inspector to learn of todays codes on the check-list!" Mr. Eagle said as he dragged the water hose to the pit and began dousing the remaining smoldering embers with water. Steam rose and replaced smoke. The burning was complete. The only sound was the hiss of steam…and honey bees in a box.

•14•
LIVING LIKE A KING

Kenny was up early long before Pedro and ET would arrive. He wanted plenty of time to enjoy one of his grandmother's warm biscuits, smothered in honey before heading to school.

"What is that phrase that, Mr. Eagle uses?" grandmother asked.

"When you're eating honey, you're living like a king!" Kenny raised his biscuit high to let the light sparkle through the honey. Some honey drizzled off one side and onto his chin, then his unbuttoned collar, and then landed on his pants leg -- Kenny's finger swirled up the gooey stuff and was quickly hid in his mouth -- his tongue swirled around his finger. "Liquid gold!" said Kenny. Kenny drizzled honey on one of his fingers, "Come here, Blondie!"

Blondie came up. Her tongue quickly found the sweet stuff and lapped Kenny's finger clean, then she reached and gave Kenny a big slobbery lick across his mouth. "Ah, a kiss!" Kenny laughed.

THE END

Appendix

I will liftt up mine eyes unto the hills, from whence commeth my help. My help cometh from the Lord, which made heaven and earth. He will not suffer they foot to be moved: he that keepeth thee will not slumber. Behold, he that keepeth Isreael shall neither slumber nor sleep. The Lord is thy keeper: the Lord is thy shade upon thy right hand. The sun shall not smite thee by day, nor the moon by night. The Lord shall preserve thee from all evil: he shall preserve thy soul. The Lord shall preserve thy going out and thy coming in from this time forth, and even for evermore.

PSALMS 121, KING JAMES VERSION

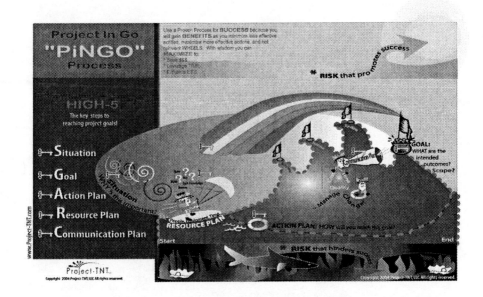

PINGO
Tools, Knowledge, Techniques

The PINGO **Methods** use proven project management practices that are of benefit to those with **Projects In Go**als.

The PiNGO **Song**... reinforces the fact that good work can be like children's play.

The PiNGO **Map**... helps users to understand both the context and the details of working towards a goal.

The PiNGO **Tools**...ensures you don't take actions on a have-baked idea but a thought through plan for project goals. Templates allow individuals and teams to jump-start performance and align mission to expectations as the project ball is moved forward to success.

PINGO Song

There was a Principle had a goal,
And PINGO was its name-o.
P -I-N-G-O!
P -I-N-G-O!
P -I-N-G-O!

And PINGO was its name-o!

There was a Principle had a goal,
And PINGO was its name-o.
(Clap)-I-N-G-O!
(Clap)-I-N-G-O!
(Clap)-I-N-G-O!

And PINGO was its name-o!

There was a Principle had a goal,
And PINGO was its name-o.
(Clap, clap)-N-G-O!
(Clap, clap)-N-G-O!
(Clap, clap)-N-G-O!

And PINGO was its name-o!

There was a Principle had a goal,
And PINGO was its name-o.
(Clap, clap, clap)-G-O!
(Clap, clap, clap)-G-O!
(Clap, clap, clap)-G-O!

And PINGO was its name-o!

There was a Principle had a goal,
And PINGO was its name-o.
   (Clap, clap, clap, clap)-O!
   (Clap, clap, clap, clap)-O!
   (Clap, clap, clap, clap)-O!

And PINGO was its name-o!

There was a Principle had a goal,
   And PINGO was its name-o.
   (Clap, clap, clap, clap, clap)
   (Clap, clap, clap, clap, clap)
   (Clap, clap, clap, clap, clap)

And PINGO was its name-o!

(Sing to the Bingo Tune)

Project-TNT, LLC
5 Par Drive, Maumelle, AR 72113
Telephone: (501) 413-9092
Fax: (810) 592-8434.
Email: TNTPress@project-tnt.com
Web: www.Project-TNT.com

Please send free information:

____ Speaking
____ Workshops
____ Consulting / Coaching
____ PINGO methods

Name: _____

Address: _____

City: _____

State: _____ Zip: _____

Telephone: _____

Email address: _____

Teresa Newton-Terres, PMP

Author, Illustrator, and
Project Management Professional

Teresa Newton-Terres is Founder and President of Project-TNT, LLC a provider of project management solutions. Teresa is a Project Management Professional (PMP®), consultant, trainer, and Fiesta enthusiast. She has extensive experience assisting individuals and the corporate world to enhance skills, reach goals, as well as develop and execute initiatives. As the Chief Imagineer of Fiesta-TNT. com, Teresa developed the project management life-skills initiative including the Recycle-Egg campaign, Diva's Team of characters, and PINGO methods in an effort to share world-class and proven practices beyond the corporate world.

Learn more at www.Project-TNT.com

Printed in the United States
66054LVS00003B/193-210

9 780979 144707